T0339484

Lecture Notes in Market Microstructure and Trading

World Scientific Lecture Notes in Finance

ISSN: 2424-9955

Series Editor: Professor Itzhak Venezia

This series provides high quality lecture note-type texts in all areas of finance, for courses at all levels: undergraduate, MBA and PhD. These accessible and affordable lecture notes are better aligned with today's classrooms and are written by expert professors in their field with extensive teaching experience. Students will find these books less formal, less expensive and also more enjoyable than many textbooks. Instructors will find all the material that they need, thus significantly reducing their class preparation time. Authors can prepare their volumes with ease, as they would be based on already existing, and actively used, lecture notes. With these features, this book series will make a significant contribution to improving the teaching of finance worldwide.

Published:

Vol. 4   *Lecture Notes in Market Microstructure and Trading*
         by Peter Joakim Westerholm (The University of Sydney, Australia)

Vol. 3   *Lecture Notes in Behavioral Finance*
         by Itzhak Venezia (The Hebrew University of Jerusalem, Israel)

Vol. 2   *Lecture Notes in Fixed Income Fundamentals*
         by Eliezer Z. Prisman (York University, Canada)

Vol. 1   *Lecture Notes in Introduction to Corporate Finance*
         by Ivan E. Brick (Rutgers Business School at Newark and
         New Brunswick, USA)

Forthcoming Titles:

Lecture Notes in Risk Management
     *by Zvi Wiener and Yevgeny Mugerman (The Hebrew University of
     Jerusalem, Israel)*

World Scientific Lecture Notes in Finance – **Vol. 4**

Lecture Notes in Market Microstructure and Trading

Peter Joakim Westerholm

University of Sydney, Australia

World Scientific

NEW JERSEY · LONDON · SINGAPORE · BEIJING · SHANGHAI · HONG KONG · TAIPEI · CHENNAI · TOKYO

Published by

World Scientific Publishing Co. Pte. Ltd.

5 Toh Tuck Link, Singapore 596224

USA office: 27 Warren Street, Suite 401-402, Hackensack, NJ 07601

UK office: 57 Shelton Street, Covent Garden, London WC2H 9HE

Library of Congress Cataloging-in-Publication Data

Names: Westerholm, Peter Joakim, author.

Title: Lecture notes in market microstructure and trading / Peter Joakim Westerholm
    (University of Sydney, Australia).

Description: 1 Edition. | New Jersey : World Scientific, [2018] |
    Series: World scientific lecture notes in finance | Includes bibliographical references.

Identifiers: LCCN 2017045440 | ISBN 9789813234093 | ISBN 9789811200465 (pbk)

Subjects: LCSH: Capital market. | Securities--Prices. | Investments.

Classification: LCC HG4523 .W47 2018 | DDC 332/.0415--dc23

LC record available at https://lccn.loc.gov/2017045440

British Library Cataloguing-in-Publication Data

A catalogue record for this book is available from the British Library.

For any available supplementary material, please visit
https://www.worldscientific.com/worldscibooks/10.1142/10822#t=suppl

Desk Editor: Shreya Gopi

Typeset by Stallion Press
Email: enquiries@stallionpress.com

Printed in Singapore

PREFACE

This book is intended to be used as basis for developing courses in securities markets, trading and market microstructure. The scope is global and the intention is to provide a framework that is relevant both for current market designs and for future markets we will see develop. This can be possible, since while market technology evolves, the role of market participants change, and whole market segments disappear to be replaced by new ways to exchange securities, the same underlying economic principles continue to drive trading in securities markets.

The book is divided into two parts. The first part contains a selection of lecture notes to be used over 10–13 teaching sessions, where students with little previous knowledge of trading will gain an in depth understanding of the mechanism that drives trading in securities markets. The lecture notes are accompanied with exercises where it is necessary to emphasize the understanding with numerical examples. For further reading and more exercises the reader is referred to a selection of suitable textbooks (Harris, 2003, Jones, 2012, and Teall, 2018). A course in securities market trading is best implemented in conjunction with a trading simulation software such as Rotman Interactive Trader [RIT], FTS, TraderEx, Interactive Brokers' IB Student Trading Lab or Stock Trak. The reader is referred to the respective websites of the developers of these programs. Another useful tool for the instructor is Bloomberg's Market Concept BMC, which allows students to qualify as a qualified Bloomberg terminal operator and to learn a wide range of important market concepts. Other information providers such as Reuters, Thomson-Reuters Datastream and Factset are very useful for student introduction to real world financial markets.

The second part of the book consists of six sessions of lecture notes for an advanced course in market microstructure theory and research. This section is largely research driven and a full list of references to research articles is provided. The second part of the book can be used to develop a series of lectures for honours or master level research students, or to develop a course for PhD students. Additional reading for this part of the book are O'Hara (1995) and Hasbrouck (2007).

I would also like to extend my thanks to Sean Foley who has provided invaluable input into developing our teaching material in trading at the University of Sydney Business School.

Sydney 2018
P. Joakim Westerholm

References

Harris, Larry, 2003, Trading and exchanges: market microstructure for practitioners, Oxford, Oxford University Press.

Jones, Charles P., 2012, Investments: analysis and management, 12 ed, John Wiley & Sons.

Teall, John L., 2018, Financial Trading and investing, Oxford, Academic Press, Elsevier.

Ohara, Maureen, 1995, Market Microstructure Theory, Cambridge, MA: Blackwell.

Hasbrouck, 2007, Empirical market microstructure: The institutions, economics, and econometrics of securities trading, Oxford University Press.

AUTHOR'S NOTE

Suggestions for professors preparing a course in market microstructure:

As part of the assessment I propose to organize assignments where students write a report based on their experience in trading sessions running one of the available trading simulation programs. A list of providers is provided in the preface to this text.

Trading Simulations: I would recommend to set aside one session or organize workshops to learn how to operate and design trading algorithms. Several of today's trading simulation programs provide such functionality.

I suggest organizing a session where students are provided and shown how to operate market information systems such as Bloomberg, Reuters and Factset. These providers have online trading programs that can be assigned for students to complete outside of class.

The second part of this volume contains five lectures based on our advanced research driven course for honors and research students.

CONTENTS

PART 1

SECURITIES TRADING
AND MARKETS

INTRODUCTION LECTURE IN TRADING IN SECURITIES MARKETS AND ADVANCED MARKET MICROSTRUCTURE THEORY — THE ECONOMICS OF TRADING

The aims of this lecture are:

This lecture puts the topic of trading in securities markets into a bigger context of financial economics and relates the current topic to what we know about capital markets, asset pricing and behavioral finance.

The purpose of this introductory lecture is to show how important it is to understand the detail of the trading process in order to explain how securities markets are organized within international capital markets to provide price discovery, liquidity and lower costs of transacting and obtaining information.

To provide a more balanced argument regarding conceptions about trading as a zero sum game where behaviorally biased individual investors are taken advantage of by large institutional investors.

Having discussed these topics it should be clear to both professor and student that market microstructure has a theoretical rigor that has its place among the other areas of mainstream finance and economics.

At the end of this lecture you should be able to answer:

— Why do we have secondary markets for financial assets where they are traded (ownership changes hands) continuously almost 24 hours a day?
— What are the main types of market participants and what are the objectives of their trading?
— What makes investors trade?

Source: Industry specialists and a famous academic study in *Journal of Finance*.

Investments is the study of the process of committing funds to one or more assets.

Why Study Investments?

— Most individuals make investment decisions sometime.
— Essential part of a career in the following fields: security analyst, portfolio manager, registered representative (broker/market maker), Certified Financial Planner, Chartered Financial Analyst, trader.
— Any level of expected return (ER) and risk can be attained.

Investors manage risk at a cost = lower expected returns.

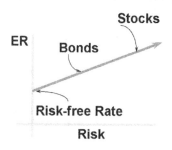

A note from the finance professional

The investment decision is a two-step process:

1. Security analysis and valuation of individual securities: necessary to understand security characteristics
2. Portfolio management
   — Selected securities viewed as a single unit (portfolio)
   — How efficient are financial markets in processing new information?
   — How and when should it be revised?
   — How should portfolio performance be measured?

Investment objectives:

— Safety of Principal
— Growth of Principal
— Current Income
— Tax Protection
— Inflation Protection

Investment alternatives: Non-marketable Financial Assets

— Commonly owned by individuals
— Represent direct exchange of claims between issuer and investor
— Usually very liquid or easy to convert to cash without loss of value
— Examples: savings accounts and bonds, certificates of deposit, money market deposit accounts

Forms of risk

— Business Risk
— Financial or Bankruptcy Risk
— Liquidity Risk
— Political Risk
— Economic Risk
— Systemic Risk

Money Market Securities

— Short-term (<1 year), liquid, relatively low risk debt instruments
— Government bills, bank certificates and commercial paper

Capital Market Securities

— Marketable debt with maturity greater than one year and shares

Derivative Securities, Options, Futures, Swaps and Hybrids

Economic functions of Financial Assets: (1) transfer of surplus funds to those who need to invest in tangible assets (2) distribute the risk of cash flows generated by tangible assets.

Economic functions of Financial Markets: (1) determine the price and at the same time the required rate of return of Securities/Financial Instruments (2) provides a mechanism to sell Securities. (3) reduce the costs of transacting, search costs and information costs.

Globalization of Financial Markets: Entities seeking to raise funds need not be confined to the domestic market; investors are not limited to financial assets issued in their home country. Factors that have led to the integration of financial markets are (1) deregulation and liberalization, (2) technological advances for monitoring, executing orders and clearing in global markets, and (3) increased institutionalization of financial markets.

Financial Innovation: Since the 1960s there has been a surge in financial innovations:

1. Market broadening instruments, new opportunities to invest and borrow (junk bonds, leveraged buyouts (LBOs), hedge funds, exchange-traded funds (ETFs), algorithmic and high-frequency trading)
2. Risk-management instruments
   (futures, options, swaps, netted clearing)
3. Arbitraging instruments and processes.
   (FX arbitrage, arbitrage funds, merger arbitrage, pairs trading)

Four principal financial product types

A. Equities
common stock, preferred stock, warrants

B. Fixed income securities
some preferred stock, bonds, money market instruments

C. Derivatives

options, futures, forwards, swaps, warrants

D. Money

currency and coins, deposits
> We will focus on the top three in this course.

Distinct Categories of Market Participants and the Purpose of their Trading

Financial Intermediaries (the sell side)

— Investment banks, brokerage firms, market makers, dealers
— Purpose of their trading: market presence, brokerage, liquidity provision, facilitation

Financial Institutions

— See Frino and Segara (Table 1.1, p. 4) for market share of Australian institutions (e.g. Superannuation Funds, Public Unit Trusts, Life Insurance Companies, General Insurance Companies, Cash Management Trusts).
— Purpose of their trading: to invest funds for future pension or insurance payouts, lending and financing and hedging their portfolios.

Asset Management Firms, e.g. Blackrock around \$3.8 trillion under management!

— Purpose of their trading: Invest client fund actively or passively (index tracking) for management fees.
— Hedge funds: invest select large client funds aggressively for **performance fees** (examples later).

Financial Planners: Advice household clients on investments and tax.

Asset/Liability Risk Management: Concerns of regulators: (a) Credit Risk, (b) Counterparty Risk (counterparty fails obligation), (c) Liquidity Risk (counterparty late), (d) Market Risk (value-at-risk used to assess this risk), and (e) Operational Risk (failure of internal processes including legal risks) e.g. fraud, rouge traders.

Distinct Categories of Market Participants and the Purpose of their Trading

Asset/Liability Problem of Depository Institutions: earn spread between loans and deposits, faces credit risk, regulatory risk (increased reserve requirements) and interest rate risk.

Commercial Banks: lending and servicing corporations

Savings and Loans Associations: lending and servicing households (US)

Savings Banks: lending and servicing households

Credit Unions: owned by members, low fee banking services for households, alternative to banks.

Central Banks and the Creation of Money

— **Purpose**: Maintain the stability of the currency and money supply for a country or group of countries. Bank of Japan: "To issue banknotes and to carry out currency and monetary control. To ensure smooth settlement of funds among banks and financial institutions. Currency and monetary control through price stability contribute to the sound development of the economy."

— **The world listens very carefully when the Federal Reserve Chairman (Janet Yellen) speaks**: Gives indications of what is going to happen to interest rates, very important for currency, bond and stock markets.
Monetary Policy

— Influences the supply of money through (1) imposing **reserve requirements** on deposit taking institutions currently, for example, on transaction accounts 12% and short-term deposits 3% in US, and (2) **Open market operations**: buying or selling government securities for reserve's own account.

Regulation

Major Exchanges are to some extent self-regulated in the day to day monitoring of markets, but government regulators such as Securities and Exchange Commission (SEC) and Commodities and Futures Trading Commission, enact securities markets law and regulation.

Distinct Categories of Market Participants and the Purpose of their Trading

Insurance Companies: Life and General Insurance, important institutional investors, able to assess and take on long-term risks, now often blurred with banking as a result of mergers, can be highly profitable.

Investment Companies (mutual funds (US), investment funds (British)) and ETFs hold the largest proportion of funds under management in most countries. There has been a large increase in the proportion of individual's self-managed accounts recently.

— Allow investors to invest in shares/units in a diversified portfolio at low costs and leave the management of the portfolio to the fund; has gained in popularity.
— Investment funds are used by more hands-off investors.
— ETFs by self-managing investors, who can invest in all kinds of markets and financial assets through these funds.

Pension Funds (Internationally) and Superannuation Funds (Australia)

— The largest group of institutions in some countries (Australia: >53%).

Important

THE MAJOR COUNTERPARTIES TO INSTITUTIONAL INVESTORS ARE:

Corporations, listed and private:

— Transferring their risks and financing needs to investors through financial intermediaries
— Investing in tangible assets and businesses.

Private Individuals and Households

— Investing savings and pension funds for future consumption
— Borrowing funds for housing and consumption.
— Sometimes households are as an aggregate group able to take on more risk and usually invest more long term than institutions
— Often takes the opposite side of institutional traders (either intermediaries provide liquidity to households or households provide liquidity to institutions).

Connecting to Corporate Finance and other Common Finance Classes

Pricing of Financial Assets: Price = PV (future cash flows)

The Level and Structure of Interest Rates: Driven by outlook of economy, currency supply/demand and central bank manipulation of interest rates.

The Term Structure of Interest Rates: Short-term rates affected by monetary policy, long-term rates based on market expectations.

Risk/Return and Asset Pricing Models: CAPM, Black & Scholes, the Cost of Carry Model.

LEARN MORE IN CORPORATE FINANCE, DERIVATIVE SECURITIES AND FIXED INCOME UNITS OF STUDY!

We will be using these models to price futures and options when we look for mispricing (arbitrage opportunities) in this unit.

A note from the finance professional

What are the incentives that drive investors/traders? Important distinction:

A. Trade to take advantage of short-term movements in asset prices
OR

B. Invest to create a well-diversified portfolio that provides the expected rate of return at the suitable level of risk.

Do not mix the two, never leave a trade in the portfolio just because it did not work and try to justify it as a long-term investment for diversification!

1. Decide what your purpose for trading in the market is, short-term speculation, diversification, value, arbitrage, hedging, liquidity provision
2. Device a strategy: Fundamental, Technical, Momentum, Contrarian
3. No clear purpose for trading, no clear strategy will lead to losses! IF SO:
4. Invest in the index — leverage for more risk, make fixed income deposit for less risk. ETF on index is today the most affordable way of indexing!

What Are Behavioral Biases and Who is Impacted?

Grinblatt and Keloharju [2001] study a large sample of investors of all types, institutions, households, corporations, government and non-profit organizations.

They analyze determinants of buy and sell transaction in a large sample of investors and find that

— Past Returns (larger positive past return is positively related to sell decision)
— Reference Price (purchase price affects the decision to sell)
— Capital Gain or Loss (reluctant to take large losses, too eager to take small profits)
— Length of Holding Period (longer holding period less affected by reference price and past returns)
— Tax Loss Selling
— The smoothing of consumption over the life cycle

are ALL determinants of the decision to trade, households being more biased.

Concludes that current theoretical models are not sufficient to explain these behavioral biases.

Are Individual Investors and Households Uninformed?

Recent research has found that **the classical view that individual household investors are naive, noise traders appears incorrect.**

— In the short run (1 month), households are rewarded for providing liquidity to institutions (Leung, Rose and Westerholm [2012]; Kelley and Tetlock [2012]; Grant, Mills and Westerholm [2014]).

— In the long run (>1 year), contrarian households are rewarded for being on the opposite side of asset pricing bubbles like the tech boom of 1998/2000 and the Global Credit Crisis (2007/2009) (see Westerholm, Swan and Lu [2014]).

— Institutional fund managers follow the signal of aggregated retail buys–sells and are trading profitably around the world on this signal (Financial industry source [2012]).

Is Investing and Trading a Zero Sum Game?

It has been argued that trading is a **zero sum game**, for you to be able to make a profit someone else has to lose this money to you. When trading is costly, this would lead to most traders losing money!

This is not quite true, in the short run, say one trading day if all traders opened their positions in the morning and closed them at night, then the wins would sum up to the losses less costs (day traders, short-term FX trading, highly leveraged margin trading in shares).

Investors and traders have many **diverse reasons for trading** and very **different holding periods**, hence it is possible that one trader takes a short-term loss, but benefits from the risk transfer to another trader who makes a short-term gain for taking on this risk.

There are also **situations when all/most traders are better off**, for example, when the share markets rise due to better profits from corporations, this benefits both short- and long-term traders (while those that have bet on falling prices make a loss in the short-term at least).

What investment/trading strategy one follows is a very personal choice.

What Trading Strategy Will You Use?

Disclaimer: The instructors of this unit of study are not licensed to give you investment advice and you should consult a registered financial advisor in case you are interested in becoming engaged with investing and trading in securities. Information about how to find a financial advisor can typically be found on the website of Securities Exchanges and the market regulators.

Stock Brokers and Futures Market Participants Australia

Examples of Typical Trading Problems

Retail trades

An individual investor Jane has $6,000 to invest. It is Friday July 24, 2015.

Jane thinks the upcoming earnings released by Facebook (FB) is going to be a good news and wants to add FB to her portfolio, and decides to buy 50 shares. Stock is trading around $96.95, up by 1.51 from the close the previous day.

— Solution: enter a limit buy order to buy 50 shares at $96.95 into the online brokerage system. The value of the trade if executed is $4,847.5.

Jane also thinks that her portfolio needs to contain search engine and software giant Google, but thinks the stock is quite expensive, $623 a share, she can afford only one share.

— Solution: enter an order to buy one (1) September 625 call option and to write (−1) September 650 call option. This is a bull spread with the following investment and payoff. These options expire on September 18, so there is a limited time for this investment, and all invested capital is lost if the share stays at current level or falls in price.

— **Investment**: outlay: 1×22.50 (contract price) $\times 100$ (underlying shares) $= \$2,250$, income: 1×10.00 (contract price) $\times 100 = -\$1,000$, total investment $1,250$ plus commissions.

— **Payoff**: if share goes above 650 by September 18.

$$650 - 625 = 25 \times 100 = \textbf{\$2,500,}$$

profit $1,250 less commissions (if you bought one stock at $623 and sold at $650 profit is **$27**, with lower risk and no time limit!).

Fundamental Information is Very Important for Investors and Traders

Investors get important cues for future cash flow and growth from earnings releases. Some speculate on the direction of the actual release compared to expectations, as surprises may lead to drastic price changes.

Zacks Equity Research: Social networking giant **Facebook, Inc.** (FB) was set to report its second quarter 2015 earnings on July 29, 2015. While the company reported a negative surprise of 4.17% in the previous quarter, it is noteworthy that over the preceeding four quarters it had a positive earnings surprise of 2.05%. It had outgrown many industry majors to be in the league of Google GOOGL and Amazon.com Inc. AMZN. (http://finance.yahoo.com/news/facebook-earnings-glow-amzn-nflx-201408179.html)

Options quotes can be obtained from, for example, Yahoo Finance. Traders usually use their broker's online trading platform for this purpose.

	BID	ASK	VOLUME	OPEN INTEREST
Sep 2015 625 CALL	**21.70**	**22.50**	58	241
Sep 2015 650 CALL	**9.00**	**10.30**	25	100

Examples of Typical Trading Problems

Institutional trades

The portfolio manager of an institution Super Fund Plc wishes to increase the weight of Newcrest Mining (ASX: NCM) — one of the largest gold mining stocks — in their portfolio by 3% as the gold price has started to rise. The institution is currently holding 1 million shares worth 19.3 million AUD.

Solution:

— The Super Fund's trader James would pull up the online access system IRESS they have through one of the many brokerage firms they use for their investments to see what the current situation in NCM is, he sees (OVERLEAF):

— At 3 p.m. in the afternoon, 2,797 shares at 19.38 and 1,000 at 19.47.

— James quickly estimates that they need to purchase 0.03×1 million $= 30,000$ shares of NCM. At the moment the depth at the best offer price is only 2,797 shares!

— James calls up one of the Institutional Investment Bank (say UBS) they use to find out what is the best they can offer 10,000 shares of NCM at.

— James also calls his contact at Macquarie Bank and asks them to put in an order for 30,000 shares of NCM into the Australian Stock Exchange dark pool (CENTRE POINT).

Why? What is James trying to achieve? Why doesn't he buy what is available in the market, about 5,000 shares? Why does he ask for 10,000 shares only? Why two brokers? What is a dark pool?

Why?

— What is James trying to achieve?

Minimize the market impact of his relatively large order (the order size is approximately 1% of the daily volume of 62.8 million dollars in total).

— Why doesn't he buy what is available in the market, about 5,000 shares?

James decides it is not wise to directly start buying in the market as this may temporarily lead to higher prices for the some of the stocks he is trying to buy.

— Why does he ask for 10,000 shares only from UBS?

James does not wish to expose his full interest to one broker as this may provide him with a better price as UBS does not see how much he really needs (remember these tactics may have negative impact on the relationship between broker and customer if misused).

— Why two brokers?

It is always good to have several brokers competing for your business to maximize price improvement.

— What is a dark pool?

One of the latest options in trading venues is to route orders to a dark pool where orders can be executed with less exposure to other traders, and hence may receive price improvements as compared with the "lit" main ASX market where all orders are visible pre-trade.

Wealthy and Successful Entrepreneurs

To gain a perspective of wealth: Who is/was_Wealthier?

John D. Rockefeller

In 1870, he founded the Standard Oil Company and ran it until he officially retired in 1897. By the 1880s, Standard Oil Company's share of the world oil refining topped out above 90% but slowly dropped to about 80% for the rest of the century.

By 1937, John D. Rockefeller had a personal wealth of $1.3 billion. He was the world's first billionaire.

Bill Gates

In 1975, he cofounded Microsoft and ran it as CEO until he officially retired in 2000. Microsoft is one of the world's largest software companies with revenue of $93.58 billion in 2015.

By 2015, Bill Gates had a personal wealth of $79.2 billion. He is hence one of the world's richest people.

Is Bill Gates richer than Rockefeller?

John D. Rockefeller is considered by many to be the wealthiest person **ever**. If he was able to maintain his wealth at the rate of inflation, which has averaged 3.6% p.a. in nominal terms since 1937, then by 2015 his wealth would have been **$21.8 billion**. Given his wealth comprised mainly common stock, he might have been able to maintain it at the rate of return of the S&P Composite Index, which since 1937 has averaged 9.55% p.a. in nominal terms, then by 2015 his wealth would have been **$1.6 trillion**.

COMPARE
Bill Gates (Microsoft) — $90 billion
Jeff Bezos (Amazon) — $112 billion

Warren Buffet (Berkshire Hathaway) — $84 billion

The most well-known investor Warren Buffett (1930–)

$90,192,000,000 under management
Personal Net Worth: 2018, $84 billion (#3)
Holdings:
(http://www.cnbc.com/id/22130601)

- Wells Fargo
- Coca Cola
- IBM
- American Express
- Procter and Gamble
- Wal Mart Stores

Berkshire Hathaway Stock: (BRK.A fianance.google.com)

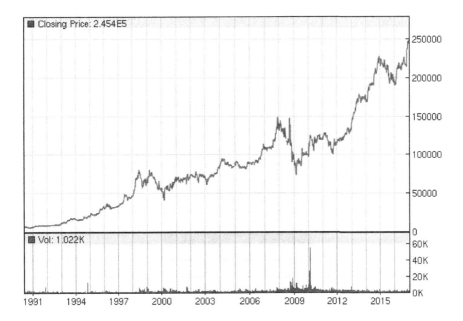

Traders and Hedge Fund Managers

One of Jones' earliest and major successes was predicting Black Monday in 1987, tripling his money during the event due to large short positions. **Paul Tudor Jones II** (1954), is the founder of Tudor Investment Corp., private investment partnerships, also referred to as hedge funds.

The industry standards are 2% p.a. of assets under management and 20% of the profits, Tudor Investment Corp. charges 4% p.a. of assets and 23% of the profits.

Contrarian attempt to buy and sell turning points.

Keeps trying the single trade idea until he changes his mind, fundamentally. Otherwise, he keeps cutting his position size down.

He trades the smallest amount when his trading is at its worst.

Considers himself as a premier market opportunist. When he develops an idea, he pursues it from a very-low-risk standpoint until he has been proven wrong repeatedly, or until he changes his viewpoint.

Swing trader, the best money is made at the market turns. Has missed a lot in the middle, but catches a lot tops and bottoms. Estimated net worth in 2018 was $4.5 billion (Forbes).

James Harris "Jim" Simons is an American hedge fund manager, mathematician and philanthropist (1938–).

His trades average typically +100% p.a.!

In 1982, Simons founded Renaissance Technologies, a private investment firm based in New York with over $15 billion under management. Simons retired at the end of 2009, as CEO, of what is widely considered the world's most successful hedge fund. Simons' net worth is estimated to be $14 billion (Forbes, underestimation?).

Simon's fund Medallion employs high frequency trading and exploits inefficiencies in the stock market. One strategy they use takes advantage of the inefficiencies in the execution of large transactions. One of their algorithms determines whether a very large order is executed and front runs it. As a result Medallion experiences high transaction costs and high expenses. That is why they charge a 5% fixed fee. On top of that they charge performance fee. That fee had been 20%, but after 2000 it increased initially to 36% and then to 44%!

The world's richest hedge fund manager though is officially **George Soros with net worth $24.9 billion!**

Soros, "broke" the bank of England trying to defend the pound, predicted and profited from the Asian crisis, orchestrated a number of other famous trades.

LET US STOP TALKING AND START EXPERIENCING WHAT TRADING IS ABOUT!

Start up your computer!

Form groups of three to four students
LOG IN to your trading simulation program and follow the instructions from your Professor.

LECTURE 1

INTRODUCTION TO SECURITIES TRADING AND MARKETS

Summary of Lecture 1

This lecture defines terms and concepts necessary to pursue studies of securities market trading and market microstructure.

After this lecture, the student will be able to take part in discussions of trading problems and start developing their own analytical skills for solving such problems.

The student will also be equipped with the terminology necessary for further reading of research articles in the area.

The lecture notes in this section are based on Teall [2012, Chapter 1], which is also recommended as further reading for this section.

A. Trades, Traders, Securities and Markets

A *trade* is a security transaction that creates or alters a portfolio position based on an investment decision.

Trade decisions concern how to execute the investment decision, in which markets, at what prices and times and through which agents.

Traders compete to generate profits, seeking compatible counterparties in trade and seeking superior order placement and timing. Trader types include:

Proprietary traders, who seek profits by trading on their own accounts.

Agency traders, who trade as commission brokers on behalf of clients.

Arbitrageurs, who focus on price discrepancies

Hedgers, who seek to control risk

Dealers, who trade directly with clients

Brokers, who seek trade counterparties for clients.

Dealers maintain quotes.

Bids, which are solicitations to purchase

Offers, which are solicitations to sell

The spread is simply the difference between the best offer and bid.

Buy side traders such as individual investors, mutual funds and pension funds buy exchange or liquidity services.

Sell side traders such as day traders, market makers and brokers provide liquidity and markets to buy side traders.

Securities and Instruments

A security is a tradable claim on assets of an institution or individual. Security types include:

Debt securities, which denote creditorship and typically involve fixed payments

Equity securities (stock), which denote ownership in a business or corporation

Derivative securities, which have payoff functions derived from the values of other securities, rates or

Call: A contract granting its owner the right to purchase a given asset

Put: A contract granting its owner the right to sell a given asset

Futures contracts, which oblige their participants to either purchase or sell a given asset at a specified price

Swaps: Provide for the exchange of cash flows associated with one asset, rate or index for the cash flows associated with another asset, rate or index

Commodities: Contracts, including futures and options on physical commodities such as oil, metals, corn, etc.

Currencies

Long and Short Positions

Spot and forward options, futures, swaps, commodities and currency contract participants take one position in each of two assets or currencies:

Long: An investor has a "long" position in that asset or currency that he will accept at the later date.

Short: An investor has a "short" position in that asset or currency that he must deliver in the exchange.

B. Securities Trading

Trading occurs in securities markets, physical or virtual, where traders communicate with one another and execute transactions.

The basic function of a market is to bring together buyers and sellers.

Four Components of a Trade

1. *Acquisition of information* and quotes

   (a) *Quality information and transparency* are crucial to price discovery.
   (b) *Transparent* markets quickly disseminate high-quality information.
   (c) *Opaque markets* are those that lack transparency.

2. *Routing* of the trade order

   (a) Selecting the broker(s) to handle the trade(s).
   (b) Deciding which market(s) will execute the trade(s) and transmitting the trade(s) to the market(s).

3. *Execution.* Buys are matched and executed against sells according to the rules of that market.

4. *Confirmation, clearance and settlement*

   (a) Clearance is the recording and comparison of the trade records.
   (b) Settlement involves the actual delivery of the security and its payment.
   (c) Might include *trade allocation.*

Algorithmic Trading

Algorithmic trading (also called automated trading, black box trading, robotrading, and often used interchangeably with high frequency trading[1]) is used to break up large orders into smaller orders to reduce execution risk, preserve anonymity and to minimize the price impact of a trade.

Hidden portions of large institutional orders are sometimes referred to as dark liquidity pools.

Orders are often partially revealed, in which case they are called iceberg or hidden-size orders.

Algo Strategies

Algorithmic trading results *from* mathematical models that analyze quotes and trades, identify liquidity opportunities, and use this information to make intelligent trading decisions.

> Some algo models seek to trade at or better than the average price over a day (e.g. volume weighted average price (VWAP)).
> Some seek to execute slowly so as to have minimal price impact.
> Algorithms sometimes are set to produce more volume at market opens and closes when volume is high, and less during slower periods such as around lunch.
> They can seek to exploit arbitrage opportunities or price spreads between correlated securities.

Algorithmic trading is also used in a more general sense to include Alpha Models, which are used to make trade decisions to generate trading profits or control risk.

Thus, more generally, algorithmic trading can be defined as trading based on the use of computer programs and sophisticated trading analytics to execute orders according to pre-defined strategies.

Algo Risks

Algorithmic trading does have the following risks:

- Leaks might arise from competitor efforts to reverse engineer them.

---

[1]High frequency trading (HFT) is one form of algorithmic trading, where the speed advantage of computers and efficient algorithms is used to decide on and execute trades very swiftly, with the intention of gaining a benefit over slower traders. Algorithmic trading is hence a broader definition of computerized trading of all forms while HFT is a sub-section of all types of algorithmic trades.

- Many algorithms lack the capacity to handle or respond to exceptional or rare events.

Thus, careful human supervision of algorithmic trading and other safeguards is crucial.

C. Bargaining

Bargaining is the negotiation process over contract terms that occurs between a single buyer and a single seller for a single transaction.

Liquidnet, an upstairs market that matches institutional buyers and sellers of large blocks of equity securities, enables institutions to directly bargain and trade confidentially with one another.

In 2008, *Liquidnet* claimed an average trade size of approximately 198,000 shares, compared to average order sizes of less than 300 shares in the NYSE and NASDAQ markets.

Bargaining Power

Bargaining power is the relative ability of one competitor to exert influence over another, and is typically a product of:

- Patience and liquidity, which increases bargaining power
- Risk aversion, which reduces bargaining power
- Credible alternatives and options that enhance bargaining power
- The cost of backing down, which decreases bargaining power
- Superior information, which increases bargaining power
- Reputation with respect to strength, staying power and resolve, all of which enhance bargaining power.

D. Auctions

The economic principle behind all financial trading is identical to the principles guiding auctions.

An *auction* is a competitive market process involving multiple buyers, multiple sellers or both.

An auction is the process of trading a security through bidding, then placing it to the winning bidder.

Vickrey [1961] demonstrated that optimal bids are increasing in bidders' values, therefore, the auctioned object will be won by the bidder who values it the most.

Auctions are a useful and cost-effective method for pricing a security with an unknown value. That is, auctions are useful price discovery processes.

A *Walrasian auction* is a simultaneous auction where each buyer submits to the auctioneer his demand and each seller submits his supply for a given security at every possible price. Thus, the Walrasian auction finds the clearing price that perfectly matches the supply and the demand.

Types of Auctions

- *English auction* or ascending bid auction
- *Dutch auction* or descending bid auction
- *First-Price Sealed-Bid* auctions have all bidders simultaneously submit sealed bids so that no bidder knows any of the other bids.

  — Does not allow for price discovery until the auction concludes. The winner submits the highest bid and pays the bid price.
  — The winner faces the *Winners Curse* problem if the auctioned item's value is not known with certainty.

- The *Second-Price Sealed-Bid auction* (Vickrey auction)

  — Identical to the First-Price Sealed-Bid auction, except that the winner pays the highest losing bid rather than his own winning bid.
  — Intended to encourage higher bids by reducing the Winner's Curse.
  — Bidders bid more aggressively because a bid raises the probability of winning without increasing the expected cost, which is determined by someone else's bid.

- *Double auction* or *bilateral auction*

Revenue Equivalence Theorem

The *Revenue Equivalence Theorem*, perhaps the most significant result from the game theory of auctions, states that, under specific restrictions, the auction type (from the listing above) will not affect the auction outcomes.

The auctioned object simply is taken by the bidder who most values it.

Common Value Auctions

In a *common value auction*, all bidders place the same value on the item to be auctioned, and that value is known with certainty.

Consider an example with three bidders where each can bid on some random amount of cash between 0 and \$1. Suppose that every monetary value between 0 and \$1 is equally likely, such that $E[V] = \$0.50$. Since each bidder has equal access to information, we will refer to this structure as a *Symmetric Information Structure* problem.

Without additional information, risk neutral bidders will value the random sum at \$0.50; risk averse bidders will value the sum at less than \$0.50.

Thus, we see here that risk aversion will affect valuation of an object of unknown value. Therefore, risk aversion will affect bids.

The Revenue Equivalence Theorem no longer applies because bids will not only be a function of expected value, they will also depend on information revealed in the bidding process.

Asymmetric Information

Next, suppose that each of the three bidders obtains a noisy signal, s_1, s_2 and $s_3 \in (0, 1)$ concerning the value such that the mean of the signal amounts equal the value of the bundle: $(s_1 + s_2 + s_3)/3 = V$.

Suppose that Bidder 1's signal is $s_1 = 0.80$. Then, his estimate of the value of the bundle is $E[V_1|s_1 = 0.80] = (\$0.80 + \$0.50 + \$0.50)/3 = \$0.60$, based on his assumption that other bidders receive signals with expected values of \$0.50. If Bidder 1 is risk neutral, \$0.60 is the value that he attributes to the bundle.

First, recall the Winner's Curse problem. If Bidder 1 wins the auction by bidding \$0.60, this will mean that the other bidders received lower value signals than Bidder 1.

Thus, winning the auction is a negative signal (*ex-post*) as to the value of the bundle; Bidder 1 will have overbid at $0.60 and will suffer from the Winner's Curse.

This means that, from the perspective of Bidder 1 if he wins, the distribution of bundle value must range from 0 to 0.80 rather than from 0 to 1.00.

The anticipated mean signal values received by other bidders should be $0.40, since their valuation ranges will be from 0 to $0.80 given that Bidder 1 will submit the highest bid.

Thus, based on this information, Bidder 1 should revise his bid for the bundle to $[B1|s_1 = 0.80] = (\$0.80 + \$0.40 + \$0.40)/3 = \$0.5333$.

Real World Examples

The opening and closing calls on our local exchange (see the Exchange website).

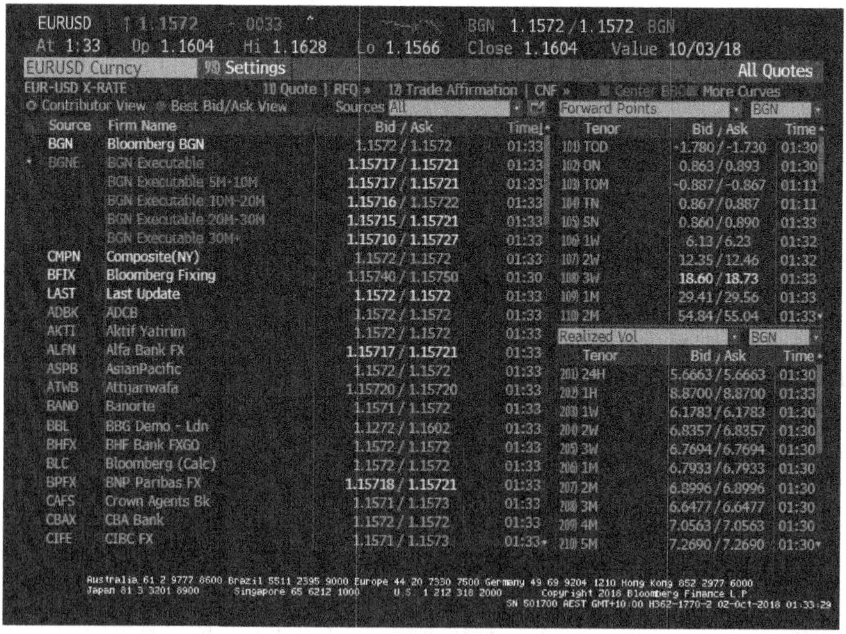

Figure 1.1: Current sample quotes from trading platforms and Bloomberg.

A live example of the current trade and quote data from the local stock exchange and a relevant commodities market (see the Exchange website or broker's trading platform).

E. Introduction to Market Microstructure

Market microstructure is concerned with the markets for transaction services.

Market microstructure concerns trading and market structure, market rules and fairness, success and failure, and how the design of the market affects the exchange of assets, price formation and price discovery.

Market microstructure is concerned with costs of providing transaction services along with the impact of transactions costs on the short-run behavior of securities prices (see Stoll [2003]). The market structure is the physical (or virtual) composition of the market along with its information systems and trading rules.

Market microstructure examines *latency*, the amount of time that lapses from when a quote or an order is placed by a trader and when that order is actually visible to the market.

Generally, the best market is that which has the lowest transactions costs, facilitates the fastest trades, results in the fairest prices, disseminates price information most efficiently and provides for the greatest liquidity.

A market is said to be liquid when prospective purchasers and sellers can transact on a timely basis with little cost or adverse price impact.

Market Execution Structures

Securities markets are categorized by their *execution systems*, that is, their procedures for matching buyers to sellers.

Quote-driven markets, where dealers post quotes and participate on at least one side of every trade (most over-the-counter (OTC) and bond markets).
Order-driven markets, where traders can trade without the intermediation of dealers (most exchanges).

Brokered markets, where many blocks are broker-negotiated.

Hybrid markets have characteristics of more than one of the above.

F. Orders, Liquidity and Depth

Orders are specific trade instructions placed with brokers by traders without direct access to trading arenas. The typical brokerage will accept and place a number of types of orders for clients. Among these types of orders are the following:

Market order: execute at the best price available in the market

Limit order: an upper price limit is placed for a buy order; a lower price limit is placed for a sell order

Stop order: buy once the price has risen above a given level; in the case of the stop sell (or stop-loss) order, the broker sells once the price of the security has fallen beneath a given level.

Day order: if not executed by the end of the day, this order is canceled

Good till canceled order: this order is good until canceled.

Not held order: here, the broker is not obliged to execute while he is attempting to obtain a better price.

Fill or Kill orders must be filled in their entirety immediately or they are canceled.

Immediate or Cancel orders are immediately executed to the extent possible; unexecuted amounts are canceled.

Liquidity

Liquidity refers to an asset's ability to be easily purchased or sold without causing significant change in the price of the asset. Black [1971] described liquidity as follows:

> "There are always bid and asked prices for the investor who wants to buy or sell small amounts of stock immediately.
> The difference between the bid and asked prices (the spread) is always small.

An investor who is buying or selling a large amount of stock can expect to do so over a long period of time at a price not very different, on average, from the current market price.

An investor can buy or sell a large block of stock immediately, but at a premium or discount that depends on the size of the block.

The larger the block, the larger the premium or discount. In other words, a liquid market is a continuous market, in the sense that almost any amount of stock can be bought or sold immediately, and an efficient market, in the sense that small amounts of stock can always be bought and sold very near the current market price, and in the sense that large amounts can be bought or sold over long periods of time at prices that, on average, are very near the current market price."

Kyle [1985] characterized three dimensions of liquidity:

Width (also known as tightness): the bid-offer spread

Depth: the market's ability to process and execute a large order without substantially impacting its price.

Slippage (also known as market impact, price impact or market resilience), which indicates the speed with which the price pressure resulting from a non-informative trade execution is dissipated (price returns to normal).

Depth

Normally, markets with larger numbers of active participants have more depth than thin markets.

Suppose, for example, that there are two competing markets for Stock X with the following offer prices (ask price in the central limit order book) for Stock X as depicted in Table 1. Suppose that the last transaction for Company X stock was at a price of $50.00. Further suppose that an investor places a market order to buy 5,000 shares of company X stock. In Market A, the investor will obtain 1,000 shares for $100.00, 2,000 for $100.30, 1,000 for $100.50 and 1,000 for $100.60.

The final price rises to $100.60. In market B, the investor will obtain 2,000 shares for $100.00, 1,000 for $100.10 and 2,000 for $100.30. The final price in Market B rises to $100.30, less than Market A. Thus, Market B has more depth than Market A, at least with respect to the stated supply of stock.

Table 1.1: Two Competing Markets
for Stock X with Varying offer Prices

MARKET A		MARKET B	
# Shares	ASK	# Shares	ASK
1,000	100.00	2,000	100.00
2,000	100.30	1,000	100.10
1,000	100.50	2,000	100.30
2,000	100.60	2,000	100.40
3,000	100.70	2,000	100.50
1,000	100.90	1,000	100.50

G. Day Trading

The Internal Revenue Service (IRS, US) defines day traders to be those who have all of the following three characteristics:

- Maintain substantial trading activity. Buys and sells frequently (e.g. 10–20 daily trades) and trading is a primary source of income.
- The trader's trading activity is sustained on a regular and continued (one year minimum) basis.
- The trader seeks to profit from short-term stock price fluctuations.

The day trader should be certain to complete a year in advance IRS Form 3115 Application for a Change of Accounting Method.

— To avoid difficulties with the wash sale rule
— To seek permission to use the mark-to-market accounting technique
— To strengthen the trader's argument that she is a for-profit day trader, allowing for better expense deduction possibilities, such as departing from the 2% miscellaneous threshold and the at-risk rules.

The Financial Industry Regulatory Authority (FINRA), based on its Rule 2520, defines the day trader to be anyone who executes buy and sell transactions on the same margin account on the same day. A *pattern day trader* executes four or more of these round-trip transactions within five consecutive business days.

Pattern day traders are required to maintain only 25% margin requirements rather than the 50% maintained by other non-institutional traders.

Rule 2520 requires maintenance of $25,000 in the margin account to take advantage of this exception, but the pattern day trader can margin this account by four times, rather than the usual two times based on the 50% rule for other individual investors.

For other individual investors, Fed Regulation T requires 50% initial margin along with maintenance margin.

Brokers

Full service brokers such as Oppenheimer, Macquarie Bank and UBS provide a wide array of services to their clients, including trade execution, advice, market research, etc.

Discount brokers such as Interactive Brokers, TD Ameritrade, E*Trade and Scottrade provide for online trade execution, and may or may not provide other services as well.

Online brokers such as Schwab, Thinkorswim and TradeKing are other discount brokers provide for online transaction order entry.

Free brokers: Robin Hood, https://www.robinhood.com/.

Direct Access Trading

In many instances, high-volume traders will require faster and better trade execution. *Direct access trading systems* may provide for faster and superior execution for such traders. Direct access trading through firms such as Interactive Brokers, Questrade and Thinkorswim enables traders to execute transactions directly with market makers and designated market makers on the NYSE, NASDAQ and ECNs, eliminating the broker from transaction participation.

The trader may have more control over routing the transaction, avoiding issues related to payment for order flow and *slippage* (movement in the security price against the trader).

Most direct access transactions execute within fractions of a second.

Direct access trading fees are typically volume-based, include exchange and other market fees, may include fixed platform and software fees. However, total fees can actually be higher than those charged by the deepest discount brokers. In addition, more knowledge is likely to be required on the part of the trader and high trading volume is likely to be necessary to make this method of trading cost-effective.

Trading Platforms

A trading platform is a computer system used to place or route quotes and transactions through a network to a financial intermediary or market.

- Trading platforms can be either software-based (e.g. TradeStation and Reuters RTEx) or web-based such as those provided by most brokers (e.g. Charles Schwab Active Trader, Thinkorswim and E*Trade).
- Software-based platforms are usually integrated with analytical tools, as are many web-based platforms.
- Trading platforms can monitor markets and can often be programmed to automatically execute trading strategies based on the customer's custom trading rules.
- Thus, the trading platform can be customized for the customer's own trading algorithms.

While trading platforms are easily obtained from brokers or developers of relevant software, there are a number of advantages to the trader creating his own platform.

- Many brokers and trading arenas are equipped to feed data into and accept quotes and execute transactions through Excel spreadsheets.
- Thus, a trader can create a spreadsheet designed to receive quotes and recent transactions data and program in his own trading rules to transmit quotes and execute transactions. Such platforms can quickly analyze market data, respond to trading rules and provide for simultaneous transmission of multiple quotes and executions. Speed, accuracy and efficiency can be enhanced with macros. For

example, macros can compare bid and offer quotes for a number of different securities, complete computations and then transmit quotes or execute transactions based on "if/then" statements reflecting trading rules.

- These macros can include buttons to follow rules, can scan data and execute transactions in the trader's absence.
- A custom spreadsheet-based trading platform is flexible and, can continue to be used when the trader switches brokers or trades new instruments.
- There are a number of firms that can assist with developing spreadsheet-based trading platforms, though many traders should be sufficiently competent to develop platforms themselves.

Trade Data

Markets usually retain ownership of market data to sell to customers. In fact, in recent years, the single largest source of revenue to the NYSE has been from the sale of price, volume and quote data.

Real time quotes are available to traders as quickly as they can be transmitted; otherwise they are said to be delayed. Delayed quotations are usually less expensive. However, in a trading environment where milliseconds (thousandths of a second) or even microseconds (millionths of a second) matter, what exactly is real time data?

In theory, real time data displays exactly as quotes are placed and transactions are executed.

However, data cannot be made available to all traders instantaneously. Data vendor services provide data using different technologies from different locations.

Traders compete to obtain data as quickly as possible and vendors compete to provide it as quickly as possible. Millisecond and even microsecond delays are to be expected, and can easily spoil many trading strategies.

More extensive real time quotations data are more expensive than less extensive data. Market data types include:

- Level I quote access displays inside quotes or Best-Bid-Offer (BBO) and, in some cases, quote sizes.

- Level II quotes display the same along with other quotes in descending order for the best bids and ascending for the best offers along with market symbols for each (see Figure 1). Level II provides the order book and is necessary for most trading strategies. While most brokers provide only Level I real time quotes for free, as of 2011, Scottrade Elite provides NASDAQ Level II and NASDAQ Total View Quotes for customers with at least 15 monthly trades while Just2Trade advertises free Level II quotes.
- Level III quotes, offered to NASDAQ members, provide direct access to enter and revise quotes. NASDAQ SuperMontage Total View provides more detail on the depth of data than Level II, enabling traders to view market makers' quotes that are not as good as their best.

Market Information Systems

One of the most popular sources of market information and price data is Bloomberg, which offers real time data and news and access to this data through its Bloomberg terminals. Costs vary but single machine access could be licensed for roughly $1,800 per month. The system provides data, news access, analytical tools, email and trade processing systems.

To learn more about how market information systems are used by market professionals see Bloomberg Market Concepts: https://about.bloomberginstitute.com/bloomberg-market-concepts/.

There are many alternatives with different focus such as Thomson Reuters, FactSetResearch Systems and Dow Jones. Less expensive quotations systems, such as eSignal and MetaStock offer prices and quotes for as little as $100 per month. For news information see Factiva.

IQFeed and eSignal provide quotes and executions to traders, and can be linked to spreadsheet trading platforms.

For a significant fee, Dow Jones and Reuters can offer electronically tagged news products that that can be picked up by computer algorithms to trigger programmed trading decisions.

Trading Arcades

A *trading arcade*, sometimes referred to as a proprietary trading firm or prop shop, is a location for traders to trade from.

The arcade might lease space, desks, trading platforms, computers and screens, analytical services, access to market data and news services such as Bloomberg or Reuters, order routing technology, clearing and settlement services and office facilities, providing for economies of scale.

Often, no physical space is provided; instead, the trader can work from her own home.

Some trading arcades will provide some or all of the capital to be traded, perhaps with or without interest. The trader can usually expect to receive reduced brokerage commissions and other trading costs. In addition, the arcade might charge for training services and receive payments from exchanges for order flow.

Some trading arcades will provide capital to traders in exchange for a split in trading profits; firms that provide capital and receive all or most of trading profits are referred to as prop shops while true arcades simply lease facilities to traders.

Many trading arcades were patronized by floor traders rendered obsolete when their trading environments transformed.

Some arcades have focused on working with amateur traders who have gone through periods of unemployment. In some cases, they have provided training to prospective traders, sometimes for a fee, after which some traders failed in their trading efforts. Trading arcades are frequently short-lived businesses, though some of the longer-lived arcades have included those operated by Jane Street Trading, Geneva Trading, London Golden Investments (LGI) and Maverick Trading.

INSTITUTIONAL TRADING

Summary of Lecture 2

These lecture notes introduce the reader to institutions, and describes their importance and market impact.

For further reading see Teall [2012, Chapter 3].

A. Institutions and Market Impact

Institutions today own the bulk of securities traded in today's marketplace and execute the majority of trades.

Institutions managed roughly \$52.1 trillion in 2009 for tens of millions of clients.

Institutional investors include buy-side institutions such as mutual funds, pension funds, life insurance companies, trust departments of banks and investment companies.

Institutional investor transactions are frequently executed by professional traders, either as employees or acting as agents, and these transactions provide opportunities and risks for other traders.

Institutional transactions also have important effects on security liquidity, prices and volatility.

For example, stocks with the largest proportional institutional ownership experience the most volatile swings when the market is most volatile. Why?

Maybe because institutions invest in larger blocks of shares and their transactions push the market more than non-institutional shareholders?

Maybe institutional shareholders are more informed than other traders? The link between institutional trading and security behavior is important to the trader.

Investment Companies

Investment company: an institution that accepts funds from investors for the purpose of investing on their behalf.

The investment company is compensated with fees, typically based on some combination of performance and investment portfolio size.

The investment company should provide professional and competent management services and pass on cost advantages resulting from economies of scale. These cost advantages include reduced transactions costs and managerial costs. In addition, these scale advantages provide for more efficient record keeping and enable improved diversification.

Institutional Trading Impact on Prices

Institutional traders can have dramatic impacts on security prices.

Institutional block buy orders result in a much larger upward effect than the downward effect caused by otherwise comparable institutional sell orders.

Why are institutional buys associated with significantly larger price impacts than institutional sells?

> "Liquidity needs drive many sales
> Most institutions have a much larger pool of stocks from which to buy than to sell
> Mutual funds are reluctant to short sell, so that they focus their research efforts on shares that they might buy and might serve as good diversification mechanisms
> Mutual funds cannot borrow to invest, so that they have to be particularly selective in their purchases." (Teall, 2012)

Thus, if one or more of these observations are correct, there should be more information content in institutional stock purchases than stock sells, and price changes will react accordingly to institutional transactions.

B. Registered Investment Companies

Registered investment companies, which are required to register with the Securities and Exchange Commission (SEC) under the Investment Company Act of 1940.

Managed investment company types:

— A *closed-end investment company* is a corporation that issues a specified number of shares that can be traded in secondary markets, such as the New York Stock Exchange (NYSE). One might purchase shares through a brokerage firm.

— An *open-end investment company*, typically known as a *mutual fund*, accepts funds directly from investors and are willing to repurchase or redeem outstanding shares. Investors buy into a mutual fund by purchasing shares and cashes out by redeeming those shares.

The major markets in which mutual funds operate are equities, fixed income, money markets and commodities and foreign exchange markets.

Money market funds seek to maintain safety and liquidity, focusing their investments in short-term, highly liquid and safe debt instruments. Such investments include US

Treasury bills and bonds, Government National Mortgage Association (GNMA), Federal National Mortgage Association (FNMA) and other federal government agency issues, bank issues such as repurchase agreements and corporate issues such as commercial paper.

Stock funds might be categorized according to their objectives or types of stock that they may invest in. Among the categories of stock funds are aggressive growth funds, growth funds, income funds, balanced funds, global funds and emerging markets funds.

Some larger fund management companies like Fidelity, Dreyfus, Vanguard and T. Rowe Price manage entire families of funds with a wide variety of investment objectives ranging from aggressive growth to generating tax-free income.

Commodity funds enable investors to take focused or diversified positions in a variety of commodities such as oil, gold and agricultural products and foreign exchange funds enable investors to take positions in the currencies and instruments of other countries.

Index Funds

Index funds employ a passive management technique where managers simply attempt to maintain a fund composition matching a particular market index (basket of stocks or other instruments) rather than attempt to "out-guess" the market.

The passive management technique is intended to keep fund management expenses low because the index strategy does not require hiring securities analysts to pick stocks in an effort to outperform the market.

Index funds provide investors with opportunities to achieve broad diversification at a low cost.

As of April 2006, total market capitalization of index funds was approximately $1 trillion, representing approximately 17% of the total equity fund market.

The share of the exchange-traded funds (ETFs) was approximately $430 billion.

Managed Investment Company Fees

Mutual funds that accept investments directly from investors without a sales charge are called *no-load* funds; investors buy and sell funds at *net asset value.*

Institutions that charge a sales fee are called *load* funds.

— The loads may be imposed when investors buy into a fund (*front-end load*), sell out of a fund (*back-end load* or redemption fee) or a combination of both.
— An investor should be aware that fund performance computations are frequently overstated because returns are usually calculated only on the investment net of fees.
— In addition, load charge percentages are generally understated in that the loads are determined as a fraction of the amount invested in the fund in addition to any loads charged.

A number of funds adopt a 12b-1 plan that enables them to use fund assets to market their shares. Such 12b-1 expenses are often included with the sum of administrative expenses when computing annual expense ratios. Funds are permitted by the Securities and Exchange Commission (SEC) to call themselves no-load funds even if they charge an annual 12b-1 fee, as long as the amount is less than 0.25% of the invested amount per year.

Load and no-load funds normally impose an annual management fee. These fees cover management compensation and various periodic administrative expenses.

Managed Investment Company Structures

A managed investment company such as a mutual fund maintains a board of directors to oversee its operations, but normally does not have managers and employees, at least not in significant numbers.

Most managed investment companies retain a separate *management company* or *advisor* to actually manage the fund's assets in accordance with the fund's prospectus. The advisor will typically hire analysts and fund managers and will pay the following types of institutions to perform certain important functions:

— *Custodian*: holds the fund assets on behalf of the shareholders
— *Transfer agent*: processes orders to purchase and redeem shares of the fund and maintains customer records. The National Securities Clearing Corporation (NSCC) processes and clears most mutual fund that involve brokers and dealers.
— *Distributor*: markets shares of the fund through various channels.

ETFs

ETFs are funds whose shares trade on exchanges.

The first was the *S&P Depository Receipt* (*SPDR* or Spider, ticker SPY) sponsored by State Street Bank and the Merrill Lynch. The Spider fund is intended to mimic performance of the S&P 500 Index by maintaining the same portfolio as the index.

Unlike the case with most mutual funds, investors can trade shares of ETFs throughout the day at market prices that vary as the market index varies. Because an ETF is not actively managed, investors can benefit from low management expenses. On the other hand, investors typically pay brokerage expenses to trade the fund and face a bid-offer spread.

Some ETFs are leveraged and investors have the opportunity to purchase ETFs on margin and short sell them.

ETFs are created by placing assets such as stocks or total return swap contracts into a trust. Shares of this trust are issued and listed on an exchange in the form of ETFs. Thus, the trust underlying SPDR contracts comprises a portfolio of individual stocks that replicates the S&P 500 (see https://www.youtube.com/watch?v=xZeDJ2bdBoE).

Bear funds such as the *Short S&P 500 ProShares* (ticker SH), created to enable investors to easily short the market index, comprise a combination of short positions in shares of stock and short positions in swap contracts involving shares.

Ultra ETFs (bull funds) enable investors to leverage index investments.

Ultra S&P 500 ProShares (ticker SSO) invests in combinations of shares along with long positions in shares in swap contracts to leverage its position in the market. Funds that double ($2\times$) or triple leverage ($3\times$) are most common among bull funds, but they are available with as much as $50\times$ leverage.

Other well-known ETFs include:

— *DIA* "Diamonds" that mimic the Dow Jones Industrial Average.
— *QQQ* that mimics that NASDAQ 100.
— Narrower sector and industry funds such as the *i-shares energy sector* that mimics the portfolio of Dow Jones Energy companies.

While different in structure from ETFs and index funds, unit investment trusts have been created to replicate indices. For example:

— *Diamonds*, shares of the Diamonds Trust created to replicate the Dow Jones Industrial Average.
— Spiders (Standard & Poor's Depository Receipts) track the S&P 500.

— *Midcap Spiders* track the S&P Midcap 400 Index.
— *Webs*, which track the Morgan Stanley world equity bench-mark indices were also created to trade on the American Stock Exchange (ASE).
— Combined, these four products accounted for approximately 15% of ASE volume prior to its acquisition by the NYSE.

Although these trusts are designed to track a particular index, their shares are often more volatile than the index itself. One explanation for this volatility is that there is substantial trading volume during market swings. This might suggest that traders' activities tend to increase market volatility.

Total return swaps provide for one party to swap cash flows on one basket of securities for cash flows associated with an interest rate instrument.

The combined market capitalization of ETFs is approximately $430 billion.

C. Unregistered Investment Companies

Pension funds are established by employers to facilitate and organize the investment of Employees' retirement funds.

— Pension funds in sum hold over $20 trillion in assets for their beneficiaries. More than half of working Americans participate in pension plans, representing very diverse ownership structure somewhat representative of the US population.
— Regulators, in part due to the Employee Retirement and Security Act of 1974 (ERISA) tend to discourage pension plans from taking imprudent risks.

Banks also provide professional asset management services, including trust management for clients.

— Trusts are legal entities or vehicles for enabling grantors (that set aside assets in trusts on behalf of the beneficiaries such as heirs, charities and others) to accomplish various financial goals. Banks in their roles as trustees or asset managers manage trusts

on behalf of grantors and their beneficiaries. Most banks maintain trust departments to serve as trustees.
— Private banking refers to services such as banking and investment management provided by banks to high net worth clients.

Private equity refers to asset managers that make equity investments in companies that are not publicly traded.

— Private equity markets provide funding for start-up firms, private middle-market firms, management buyouts (MBOs), leveraged buyouts (LBOs), firms in financial distress, and public firms seeking buyout financing.
— Private equity shares are not publicly traded (with a few exceptions), are illiquid and exempt from SEC registration requirements.
— Private equity firms frequently take active monitoring, management and advising roles in their portfolio firms. There are a variety of types of private equity firms, ranging from venture capital (VC) firms to hedge funds.

Hedge Funds

Hedge funds are unregistered private funds that allow investors to pool their investment assets.

To avoid SEC registration and regulations, hedge funds usually only accept funds from small numbers (often less than 100) of *accredited* investors, typically high net worth individuals and institutions.

Because most hedge funds have only a small number of managers, they typically focus their investment strategies on the expertise of a few key managers.

— Many hedge funds seek investment opportunities or niches where larger institutions are constrained due to regulatory restrictions. For example, because many banks, pension funds and other institutions cannot focus activities in the securities of distressed corporations, some hedge funds will specialize in such investments. Other funds may specialize in short sales and derivatives to hedge against market downturns and others will simply focus on searches for arbitrage opportunities.

— Hedge fund managers typically take a proportion of assets invested (2% is a norm) and another portion of profits (20% is typical) as compensation.

— While hedge funds are frequently able to report results that beat the market, investors should realize that performance results do not usually include the last several months of a hedge fund's existence, which is when a fund is most likely to fail.

Rule 144A Markets

Rule 144A markets are specifically created for institutional traders to trade unregistered securities.

— The SEC adopted Rule 144A in 1990 as an amendment to the Securities Act of 1933 to set forth rules and conditions for the trading of unregistered securities.

— Most securities issued under Rule 144A are by public firms needing to avoid the reporting requirements and delays associated with registered offerings.

— Some firms are foreign or private seeking to avoid SEC reporting and registration requirements.

Only Qualified Institutional Buyers (QIBs: institutions with investment portfolios exceeding $100 million) can purchase securities in a Rule 144A offering. Companies may have no more than 499 qualified institutional investors to retain their 144A status.

144A trading markets smaller firms' opportunities to obtain public funding without SEC scrutiny, paperwork and related delays and paperwork.

In Australia, unregulated issues can be marketed to qualified professional investors (approximately 10 million in assets or 350,000 annual income).

LECTURE 3

EXECUTION COSTS

Summary of Lecture 3

This lecture provides a detailed definition of transaction (trade execution) costs and how they are measured.

The focus is on costs of trading rather than investment return performance. This is emphasized in a discussion contrasting measures of investment performance with measures of transaction costs.

Understanding Volume Weighted Average Price (VWAP) and Implementation Shortfall (IS) are core aims of this section. When we calculate IS we focus on Commissions, Market Impact vs. midpoint on order arrival and Opportunity Cost vs. midpoint price on order arrival. We ignore delay costs (used in some applications) as these can be subjective and sufficient information is not always available.

Exercises in how to compute transaction costs with solutions are provided at the end of the lecture.

A. Execution Costs

Best execution, execution costs and price improvement

Best execution refers to traders receiving the most favorable terms available for their trades (Macey and OHara, 1997).

Brokers have a responsibility to provide their clients' best execution. Unfortunately, because many factors are needed to define the most favorable terms, best execution is not an easy concept to quantify, evaluate or enforce.

Suppose, for example, the best quotes are available in one market, but trades are more likely to execute between quotes in another market. Which market will provide for the best execution?

What if one market normally executes at a better price than another market, but takes longer with more risk?

Execution costs are important in evaluating best execution. Execution costs are the sum of:

Order processing costs
and
Market impact costs

Measuring *order processing costs* is normally fairly straightforward. These costs will normally include brokerage fees, which might account for other processing costs.

Slippage

However, *market impact* or slippage costs measurement is more problematic.

The price or market impact of a transaction, the effect that a given transaction has on the market price of a security, is particularly important for a large transaction or in an illiquid market.

When institutions execute large transactions, their buy or sell activities affect security prices, typically in a manner that increases execution costs.

While substantial, especially for large orders, these costs are not explicit, and are hence considered to be hidden or implicit.

Spreads

Investors need to track execution quality to measure the trading performance of their investment brokers.

Brokerage firms have traditionally used bid-offer spreads as a basis for charging commissions to their customers. That is, buyers frequently bought at the offer and sellers sold at the bid, with brokers pocketing the difference (spread) as their commission. This tradition is one reason that spreads are an important factor for gauging transactions costs. Many studies concerned with execution costs have used:

Quoted Spread (offer minus bid)
Half-Spread (quoted spread/2)

However, when transactions are executed inside spreads, these measures can overstate execution costs. Alternatives might include the *effective half-spread*, the difference between the actual transaction price and the midpoint of the spread.

None of these measures are likely to capture the *market impact* of a transaction, often referred to as *slippage*. That is, each transaction is likely to force the price in some direction, upwards for purchases and downwards for sales. Additional alternatives can include:

The *realized half-spread*, which is the difference between the security price at some future point in time and either the bid or offer quote. The realized half-spread (and the perfect foresight half-spread) might be particularly relevant when the transaction was executed as part of a series of transactions.

The *perfect foresight half-spread*, which is the absolute value of the difference between some future price and the trade price. This measure is also referred to as *market impact*, then typically signed so it takes a positive value for buys and negative value for sells.

See **exercises** how to calculate standard spread and execution costs at the end of this lecture.

Spread Comparisons

Numerous academic and regulatory studies have compared execution costs of different markets. Many older studies found that execution costs on NASDAQ were substantially higher than on the NYSE and that other equity markets did not compare favorably to the NYSE. Christie and Huang [1994] found that NYSE effective half-spreads averaged 7.9 cents compared to 18.7 cents on NASDAQ and that trading costs fall for firms that switch listings from the NASDAQ to either the AMEX or the NYSE. Similarly, Huang and Stoll [1995] found that 26.7% of trades on the NASDAQ were inside the spread, compared to 37.9% of trades on the NYSE. Thus, NYSE transactions were more likely to exhibit price improvement. Price improvement occurs when an order is executed a price better than the prevailing bid or offer.

These transaction cost levels are likely to have changed, and NASDAQ is today more competitive in comparison to NYSE. In addition, there is a large number of other alternative trading venues for US shares, where certain types of trades may encounter lower transaction costs.

Transaction Size and Slippage

Table 3.1 depicts a series of 20 historical transactions prices for brokerage firm on a given stock's purchases. It also depicts subsequent

Table 3.1: Transaction Prices for Brokerage firm on a given Stock's Purchases

#Purchase	Purchase Price	Subsequent Transaction	Perfect Foresight Half-Spread	Transaction Size	Correlation Spread to Size
1	50.00	50.30	0.30	1000	
2	50.26	50.30	0.04	200	
3	50.26	50.35	0.09	400	
4	50.17	50.33	0.16	600	
5	50.32	50.33	0.01	100	
6	50.41	50.46	0.05	300	
7	50.51	50.55	0.04	200	
8	50.44	50.47	0.03	300	
9	50.71	51.12	0.41	1200	
10	51.03	51.04	0.01	100	
11	50.97	50.99	0.02	200	
12	50.57	50.75	0.18	700	
13	50.71	50.74	0.03	200	
14	50.92	50.96	0.04	200	
15	51.91	50.93	0.02	200	
16	51.18	51.32	0.14	600	
17	51.71	51.76	0.05	300	
18	52.04	52.12	0.08	400	
19	52.03	52.34	0.31	1000	
20	52.30	52.34	0.04	300	
					0.989

transactions prices, from which perfect foresight half-spreads are computed. The sizes of the purchases follow, so that the broker can analyze the relationship between the perfect foresight half-spread and the transaction size.

Illustration: Slippage and the Perfect Foresight Half-Spread

Purchases by other investors are omitted in the "Purchase Price" column.

Notice that larger purchase orders tend to lead to higher perfect foresight half-spreads. This suggests that larger orders lead to greater slippage, just as we would expect.

What might be less apparent in the table is that the proportional increase in slippage increases as the proportional size of the transaction increases. That is, the relationship between slippage and transaction size is concave up.

We can analyze the relationship between the perfect foresight half-spread and transactions sizes with an ordinary least squares (OLS) regression. Suppose that the broker expects that this relationship will not be linear because it expects that the effect of transaction size on the perfect foresight half-spread to be concave up. That is, for example, the broker might expect that a single purchase transaction for 1,000 shares will cause more slippage than 10 purchase transactions for 100 shares each. To analyze this non-linear relationship, we conduct a log–log regression of the following form:

$$\log(\textit{Perfect Foresight Half-Spread})_t$$

$$= \log b_0 + b_1 \log(\textit{Transaction Size}) + \varepsilon_t.$$

This implies the following estimated relationship between the perfect foresight half-spread and transaction size:

$$\textit{Perfect Foresight Half-Spread} = v(\textit{Transaction Size})^m,$$

where b_0 serves as an estimate for v and b_1 serves as an estimate for m. These parameters b_0 and m characterize slippage, which is positive when v is positive and m exceeds 1. Higher values for b_0 and m indicate increased slippage.

Illustration: Slippage and Transaction Size Regression

Table 3.2 represents log values (base 10) for perfect foresight half-spreads and transaction sizes, and presents regression results. The log–log regression implies that $b_0 = -4.96$ and $b_1 = 1.48$; that is, v is approximately equal to 0.00001 and m is approximately equal to 1.5 (use anti-logs of b_0 and b_1 to obtain v and m). Thus, slippage, $S = vc^m = 0.00001\,c^{1.5}$ where c is transactions size. Regression results suggest that these results are statistically significant.

Table 3.2: Regression Results for Perfect Half-Spreads and Transaction Sizes

Log Perfect Foresight Half-Spread	Log Transaction Size					
		SUMMARY OUTPUT				
−0.522879	3.00000	Regression Statistics				
−1.397940	2.30103	Multiple R 0.977851577				
−1.045757	2.60206	R Square 0.956193706				
−0.795880	2.77815	Adjusted R Square 0.953760023				
−2.000000	2.00000	Standard Error 0.101914919				
−1.301030	2.47712	Observations 20				
−1.397940	2.30103					
−1.522879	2.47712	ANOVA				
−0.387216	3.07918					Signifi-
−2.000000	2.00000		df	SS	MS	F	cance F
−1.698970	2.30103					
−0.744727	2.84510	Regression	1	4.0809	4.0809	392.9	1.12419E-13
−1.522879	2.30103	Residual	18	0.18696	0.0104	
−1.397940	2.30103	Total	19	4.26787		
−1.698970	2.30103					
−0.853872	2.77815	Coefficients	t-Stat	P-value		
−1.301030	2.47712					
−1.096910	2.60206	Intercept	−4.961	−26.16	8.9E-16	
−0.508638	3.00000	X Variable	11.480	19.82	1.1E-13	
−1.397940	2.47712					

Source: Teall [2012].

The Three Components of Transaction Costs are Related and Should Add Up

Effective Spread, Realized Spread and Market Impact, are connected so that Effective Spread = Realized Spread + Market Impact. This association can be useful for assessing the accuracy of estimated cost components.

Illustration: In Table 3, analyzing a large sample of stocks from the Korean market for a one-year period shows how the difference between the measured effective spread and the market impact, using a reference point 10 trades after the measured trade, equals observed realized spread using the same reference point. A similar result is obtained using a different time period (Period 2) and a different reference point of 8 trades (not reported here).

Table 3.3: Analysis of a Large Sample of Stocks from the Korean Market for a Year

Period Buys/Sells	Effective Spread	Market Impact T+10	Observed Realized Spread T+10
			= Eff. Spread − Market Imp.
Period 1 Buys	0.02578	0.00312	0.02101
Period 1 Sells	−0.00334	−0.00265	−0.00060
Period Buys/Sells	Effective Spread	Market Impact T+8	Observed Realized Spread T+8
Period 2 Buys	0.01253	0.00142	0.01007
Period 2 Sells	−0.00281	−0.00160	−0.00115

Source: Refer to Pham, Swan and Westerholm [2017]; Boehmer, Saar and Yu [2005] for a thorough treatment of these transaction cost components.

B. Algorithmic Trading, Dark Pools and High-frequency Trading (HFT)

Algorithmic Trading, Dark Pools and HFT and the impact of these new market developments on transaction costs will be discussed in Lecture 12.

Today, we focus on Trade Execution by institutions outside of the fully computerized realm to better understand what happens inside the black box of algorithms and dark pools.

C. Stealth and Sunshine Trading

Barclay and Warner [1993] argue that if informed investors' trades are the main cause of stock price changes, large trades by informed traders would reveal their information because traders can easily discern those who execute large transactions.

However, small trades executed repeatedly will incur excessive transactions costs. Thus, informed traders will tend to fragment orders into medium-sized trades sufficiently small to disguise themselves but large enough to maintain fairly small transactions costs. This should lead medium-sized transactions to have the most significant impact on stock prices.

Thus, medium-sized orders (500 to 9,999 share orders) will be most likely to move stock prices if stealth traders are most active. Several empirical studies support this argument, including that of Barclay and Warner who find that 99.43% of the cumulative price changes on the NYSE result from medium-sized trades, which comprise 38.12% of total NYSE trades.

Chakravarty [2001] confirms that the bulk of price changes are due to medium-sized trades, finds that the bulk of these price-moving trades are executed by institutions and determines that the bulk of stealth trades are executed by institutions.

In contrast, Campbell *et al.* [2009] found that that institutions tend to execute larger and smaller transactions rather than medium-sized transactions.

However, the Campbell *et al.* [2009] study was more recent and the exchanges have consistently been reporting smaller average transactions sizes. Perhaps, significantly reduced transactions costs have made execution of smaller transactions less costly, leading institutions to execute an increased number of smaller transactions

Furthermore, Campbell *et al.* also found that institutions prefer medium- and small-sized trades on high volume days and larger size trades on high volatility days. Larger transactions move prices more on high volatility days. This suggests that stealth trading increases when liquidity is high, but when volatility is high, traders act more quickly with larger size trades, engaging less in stealth trading, causing their trades to move prices more.

Chakravarty, Kalev and Pham [2005] found that stealth trading occurs differently in bear markets from how it occurs in bull markets. While they did find that informed traders execute smaller trade sizes when selling than when buying, informed investors fragmented their trades more when buying in rising markets and when selling in falling markets.

Sunshine Trading

Sunshine trading is the opposite of stealth trading; sunshine traders announce their intentions. The sunshine trader announces its intentions when doing so might be expected to increase the competition to act as counterparties.

Sunshine trading is most effective when the market for the security is elastic; that is, when a larger number of competitors on the same side of the transaction might be expected to have little long-term impact on the price of the security. Even if the announcement produces a short-term impact, in an elastic market, the price will bounce back.

If information motivating a trade has already been leaked, the institution might publicize its intentions in an effort to obtain a larger number of providers of liquidity. That is, the institution might prefer to execute its transactions in a more liquid market. In fact, the signaling effect of sunshine trading might actually "scare off" potential competitors on the same side of the transaction, leading to reduced trading by competing informed traders.

Consider, for example, the 2011 scenario when the US government announced its intent to sell bank shares accumulated in its efforts to mitigate the effects of the 2008 banking crisis. The market was well aware of the US government's holdings and its intent to eventually sell the shares. Hence, when these shares ultimately were sold, the government's announcement of the anticipated sales prevented suspicions leading to unwanted negative information effects.

D. Trade Evaluation and VWAP

VWAP is calculated by dividing the dollar volume of trading in a stock by the share volume over a given period of time, typically one day.

Arrival Price: The midpoint of the bid-offer spread at the time the order is received (Bid-Ask Midpoint or BAM).

MOC (Market-on-close): the last price obtained by a trader at the end of the day relative to the last price reported by the exchange.

IS: the performance difference between the hypothetical profits realized by a paper or theoretical portfolio replicating an actual portfolio ignoring friction costs and the profits realized by the actual portfolio.

VWAP

VWAP can be used as a benchmark to evaluate the quality of the execution provided by a broker.

"If the brokerage firm's purchases were made at a lower VWAP than the market VWAP for the relevant period, the firm handled the order well for the customer."

VWAP, either for selection of trades or for the market as a whole is calculated as follows:

$$VWAP = \frac{\sum_j Q_j P_J}{\sum_j Q_J},$$

where Q_j is the quantity of shares traded for a given order j at price P_j. VWAP is the average execution price for a series of trades or a time period typically a day or sometimes several days.

VWAP: A Simple Illustration

Suppose that a broker has been instructed to purchase 600 shares at the market. She does so, purchasing them for a total price of 30,011.

The broker's executed transactions were the second through fourth transactions on the table. The total volume of shares exchanged was 2,500, with a total value of 125,098.

Hence, VWAP for these transactions was $125{,}098/2{,}500 = 50.0392$. The broker purchased 200 shares in the first transaction at 50.01 and 400 shares in the third transaction at 50.02.

The average share price paid by the broker was $30,010/600 =$ 50.0167.
Our calculations suggest that the broker beat the market VWAP.

Price	Volume	Price × Volume
50.01	200	10,002
50.01	100	5,001
50.02	400	20,008
50.02	100	5,002
50.03	200	10,006
50.05	600	30,030
50.06	400	20,024
50.05	500	25,025
Total	2,500	125,098

Implementation Shortfall

The implementation of an investment strategy by the trader or portfolio manager leads to four primary types of friction costs:

Broker, exchange and other explicit fees and commissions. Frequently, brokers bundle exchange, SEC and other fees into their own commissions. Small transactions tend to have higher proportional explicit transactions costs.

Price impact costs associated with transaction executions (slippage). Buy orders will exert upward price pressure on the security; sell orders will exert downward pressure. Larger transactions will tend to have larger impact costs.

Opportunity costs associated with transactions; that is, the opportunities and profits were forgone prior to the trade's completed execution. Opportunity costs can also include the portion of an order that was canceled due to a limit order restriction.

Delay costs are estimated in some applications, based on the price difference between the portfolio manager's decision price and the broker's arrival price, if such information is available.

Calculating Implementation Shortfall

Suppose that a portfolio manager makes a decision to purchase 10,000 shares of stock one hour before its open with a limit order at 50.45.

The stock opened at 9:30 at a price of $50.20, and 1,000 shares are purchased at 9:31 at a price of 50.25.

At 9:35, 5,000 shares are purchased for $50.40, and 1,000 more for $50.30 at 10:25.

An additional 1,000 shares are purchased for $50.30 at 13:16, the market price quickly rises to $50.48 and closes at $50.50 with 2,000 shares in the order unexecuted.

The commissions, including all explicit fees were $0.01 for each of 8,000 shares.

Time t	Volume	Price $t(\$)$
Close Previous Day		50.00
Open		50.20
9.31	1,000	50.25
9.35	5,000	50.40
10.25	1,000	50.30
13.16	1,000	50.35
Close		50.50
Commissions	$8,000 \times 0.01$	80
Price Impact	$0.05 \times 1000 + 0.20 \times 5000$ $+ 0.10 \times 1000 + 0.15 \times 1000$	1,300
Opportunity Cost	$50.50 - 50.20 \times 2,000$	600
Total Costs		1,980

E. Evaluating Investment Performance vs. Trade Execution Performance

The trade execution performance evaluation measures above are NOT to be confused with the measures of investment performance commonly applied by investment professionals based on neoclassical finance theory.

- Net asset value [NAV] performance of the simple buy and hold into a diversified portfolio strategy: Commonly used to evaluate mutual fund performance.
- Portfolio Benchmarking: Higher returns are generally associated with higher risk, such that appropriate benchmarking is important. Portfolio managers often standardize returns volatility using the Sharpe Ratio or the Treynor Ratio.
- Most commonly portfolios are evaluated fitting a Fama–French [1993] three factor model or extensions to this including, for example, Carhart's [1997] momentum factor. The "alpha" a portfolio generates when the portfolio returns are adjusted for known risk factors is used to evaluate performance.
- Market Timing vs. Investment Selection is also evaluated using methods such as the quadratic variable approach and the dummy approach.
- Value at Risk [VaR] is commonly used to manage risk exposure of investment portfolios. VaR measures the worst loss for a given time frame, with a given set of distributional assumptions at a given confidence level. VaR = *Asset Value× Daily Return Standard Deviation × Confidence Interval Factor × Square Root of Time*

$$\text{VaR} = \text{Asset Value} \cdot \sigma \cdot z \cdot \sqrt{t}$$

The results from the above methods should correctly be adjusted both for implicit and explicit transaction costs to evaluate if the performance is persistent when implementation costs are considered.

Exercises

Execution Cost Measures (metrics)

These exercises show how transactions costs commonly used by professional traders, exchanges and regulators are calculated. For further details see, for example, the research article by Bessembinder [1997]. These exercises distinguish between

- Explicit Costs such as brokerage fees and taxes, and
- Implicit Costs such as bid ask spreads and market impact

Solutions are provided at the end of this text.

Solve These Problems to Better Understand How Transaction Costs are Calculated

1. At 10:00 a.m. you observe BHP listed on the ASX. The best bid price is $26.00 and the best ask price is $24.00. What is the dollar and percentage bid-ask spread? What is the effective spread?
2. At 10:30 a.m. you observe BHP again. The best bid price is $25.49 and the best ask price is $25.50. What is the dollar and percentage bid-ask spread? What is the effective spread?
3. You are a broker at a leading brokerage firm. A client has asked you to purchase 10,000 shares in AMZN (NYSE). The current bid and ask prices are $795.50 and $795.60, respectively. The buy and sell schedules are as follows:

	Volume	Bid Price ($)	Ask Price ($)	Volume
Best Price Level	700	795.50	795.60	500
Level 2	2,000	795.40	795.70	1,000
Level 3	7,500	795.30	795.80	5,000
Level 4	12,500	795.00	796.00	10,000
Level 5	33,000	794.50	797.00	25,000

(a) What will be the average traded price if you decide to trade the entire order immediately?

(b) How does this compare with the current market price?

(c) What will the market price be following this trade?

(d) What alternative strategies may the trader employ in order to attempt to minimize this market impact?

4. You receive a large order to sell 500,000 shares in IBM. You complete the following trades:

Time	Price	Quantity
10:22:03	109.02	220,000
14:03:41	109.15	84,000
15:09:33	108.98	8,000
15:50:54	109.20	8,000

If the VWAP for IBM for that day was $109.04, how does your VWAP compare with the market VWAP?

5. You have received an order to buy stock in BOFI. Over the next two minutes the following series of trades take place:

Time	Price	Quantity
11:15:00	29.40	4,000
11:15:47	29.39	3,200*
11:16:03	29.40	900
11:16:21	29.40	600
11:16:33	29.40	8,800*
11:16:39	29.41	2,400
11:16:53	29.42	3,600*

Your buy trades are marked with *!

(a) What is the VWAP of your buy transactions for that interval?

(b) How do your buy transactions compare with prices traded for BHP during that interval?

(c) Calculate the running VWAP at each point you execute a trade, assuming the interval during which you are assessed begins at 11:15:00.

6. A trader at the brokerage firm SBU receives an order to purchase 100,000 shares of stock PHO. At the time the order was received the market price of PHO (the midpoint of the best bid and ask

quotes) was $6.30. The trader then proceeds to execute the order. Initially the trader is able to purchase 55,000 shares at $6.35. Due to lack of liquidity the trader waits until the following day to execute an additional 30,000 shares at $6.42. Because the price has risen, the trader decides not to purchase any more shares. Five business days later ($t = 7$) the stock closes at $6.60. SBU charges brokerage of $0.02 per share. What is the IS for this trade?

LECTURE 4

MARKET FRAGMENTATION AND REGULATION

Summary of Lecture 4

This lecture continues to go deeper into how the trading process is organized in modern market, we cover exchange, alternative trading systems (ATSs) and how market fragmentation and new trading technology has impacted markets. For markets to be efficient, fair and provide the functions they are set up to fulfill, regulation is an important aspect. We discuss regulation from a broad international perspective.

A. Exchanges and Floor Markets

The Securities and Exchange Act of 1934 defined an *exchange* to be: *any organization, association, or group of persons, whether incorporated or unincorporated, which constitutes, maintains, or provides a market place or facilities for bringing together purchasers and sellers of securities or for otherwise performing with respect to securities the functions commonly performed by a stock exchange as that term is generally understood, and includes the market place and the market facilities maintained by such exchange.*

An exchange is a physical or virtual meeting place drawing together brokers, dealers and traders to facilitate the buying and selling of securities.

Exchanges include the floor-based markets as well as many virtual meeting sites and screen-based systems provided by *Electronic Communication Networks (ECNs)*.

Exchange Functions

Exchanges are intended to provide for orderly, liquid and continuous markets for the securities they trade. A continuous market provides for transactions that can be executed at any time for a price that might be expected to differ little from the prior transaction price for the same security.

In addition, exchanges traditionally serve as *self-regulatory organizations* (SROs) for their members, regulating and policing their behavior with respect to a variety of rules and requirements.

Largest Exchanges in the World

Rank ◆	Exchange ◆	Economy ◆	Headquarters ◆	Market cap ◆ (USD bn)	Monthly trade volume ◆ (USD bn)
1	New York Stock Exchange	United States	New York	19,223	1,520
2	NASDAQ	United States	New York	6,831	1,183
3[2]	London Stock Exchange Group	United Kingdom Italy	London	6,187	165
4	Japan Exchange Group – Tokyo	Japan	Tokyo	4,485	402
5	Shanghai Stock Exchange	China	Shanghai	3,986	1,278
6	Hong Kong Stock Exchange	Hong Kong	Hong Kong	3,325	155
7	Euronext	European Union	Amsterdam Brussels Lisbon London Paris	3,321	184
8	Shenzhen Stock Exchange	China	Shenzhen	2,285	800
9	TMX Group	Canada	Toronto	1,939	120

Rank ⬥	Exchange ⬥	Economy ⬥	Headquarters ⬥	Market cap ⬥ (USD bn)	Monthly trade ⬥ volume (USD bn)
10	Deutsche Börse	Germany	Frankfurt	1,762	142
11	Bombay Stock Exchange	India	Mumbai	1,682	11.8
12	National Stock Exchange of India	India	Mumbai	1,642	62.2
13	SIX Swiss Exchange	Switzerland	Zurich	1,516	126
14	Australian Securities Exchange	Australia	Sydney	1,272	55.8
15	Korea Exchange	South Korea	Seoul	1,251	136
16	OMX Nordic Exchange	Northern Europe, Armenia	Stockholm	1,212	63.2
17	JSE Limited	South Africa	Johannesburg	951	27.6
18	BME Spanish Exchanges	Spain	Madrid	942	94.0
19	Taiwan Stock Exchange	Taiwan	Taipei	861	54.3
20	BM&F Bovespa	Brazil	São Paulo	824	51.1

NYSE Euronext

NYSE Euronext, the world's largest exchange and its first global exchange lists over 8,000 issues (excluding European structured products) from 55 countries on six equities exchanges and six derivatives exchanges in six countries.

NYSE Euronext was launched on April 4, 2007; the result of a merger between the New York Stock Exchange Group and Euronext, NV.

US Stock and Options Exchanges

NYSE Amex LLC (formerly the American Stock Exchange)
BATS Exchange, Inc.
BATS Y-Exchange, Inc.
NASDAQ OMX BX, Inc. (formerly the Boston Stock Exchange) C2
Options Exchange, Incorporated
Chicago Board Options Exchange, Incorporated
Chicago Stock Exchange, Inc.

EDGA Exchange, Inc.
EDGX Exchange, Inc.
International Securities Exchange, LLC
The NASDAQ Stock Market LLC National Stock Exchange, Inc.
New York Stock Exchange LLC
NYSE Arca, Inc.
NASDAQ OMX PHLX, Inc. (formerly Philadelphia Stock Exchange)

An International Case Study: Australian Trading Venues

The Australian Stock Exchange (ASX) is Australia's main listing venue.

It also undertakes the secondary trading of stocks, and the clearing and settling functions for all Australian securities.

Chi-X entered the Australian market in 2011 and competes for the secondary trading of stocks. It currently has about 20% market share.

Chi-X Australia Market Share

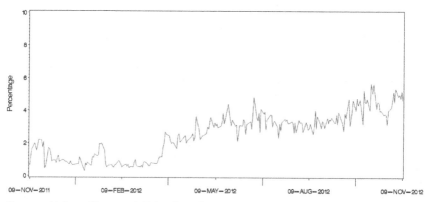

Source: Aitken, Chen and Foley [2016].

Chi-X Market Share Globally

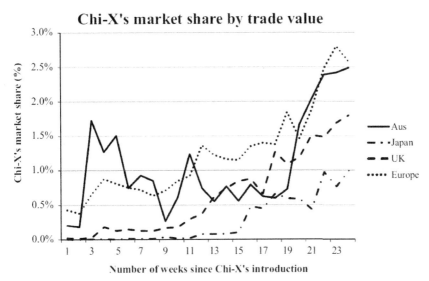

Source: He, Jarnecic and Liu [2014].

Traditional NYSE Structure

Until 2006, the NYSE was a hybrid corporation/partnership whose members faced unlimited liability.

Only members who owned or leased seats had trading privileges and there were four types of members:

— *House Broker*: Executed orders on behalf of clients submitting orders through brokerage firms. This and other broker roles have been taken over by "Trading Floor Brokers."

— *Independent Broker*: Also called a two-dollar broker, executed orders on behalf of commission brokers when activity was high. This type of distinct membership no longer exists.

— *Floor Trader*: Executed orders on their own trading accounts. The NYSE has created the "Supplemental Liquidity Provider" role, which is intended to enhance market liquidity by allowing for proprietary trading.

— *Specialist*: Responsible for maintaining a continuous, liquid and orderly market for the securities in which he specializes. The specialist has been replaced by the Designated Market Maker (DMM).

Now, under its new structure, one can join the 1,366 members by purchasing a license that permits the member to trade for 1 year.

Securities Order Routing Process

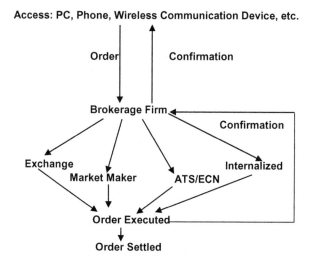

B. Over the Counter Markets and Alternative Trading Systems

The *over-the-counter markets* have traditionally been defined as the non-exchange markets.

An ATS might be loosely defined as a securities trading venue that is not registered with the SEC as an exchange.

ATS Types

Types of ATS include:

- ECNs, which are virtual meeting places and screen-based systems for trading securities.
- Dark Pools and "Crossing Networks", where quotations for share blocks are matched anonymously. Participants in crossing markets enjoy reduced transactions costs and anonymity but often must wait for counterparty orders to accumulate before transactions can be executed.
- Internalization Crossing Voice-Brokered Third-Party Matching.

Sample ATS List

Name	Host Country	Instruments	Features
Alpha	Canada	Equities	Continuous trading market
ArcaEdge	US	Equities	NYSE ATS
Chi-X Europe	UK	European Shares	Multilateral Trading Facility
Citi Match	US	Equities	Internal Crossing Network
Crossfinder	Global	Equities	Bills itself as the world's largest dark pool; Internal crossing network

ATS Definition

ATS means any organization, association, person, group of persons, or system:

1. *That constitutes, maintains, or provides a market place or facilities for bringing together purchasers and sellers of securities or for otherwise performing with respect to securities the functions commonly performed by a stock exchange within the meaning of Rule 3b-16 under the Securities Exchange Act of 1934 and 1935. That does not:*

   i. *Set rules governing the conduct of subscribers other than the conduct of such subscribers' trading on such organization, association, person, group of persons, or system; or*

ii. *Discipline subscribers other than by exclusion from trading.*

What the ATS does *not* do is what distinguishes it from an exchange.

US Equity Trading Centers Volume 2009

NYSE 14.7%
NYSE Arca 13.2%
NASDAQ 19.4%
NASDAQ OMX BX 3.3%
Broker-Dealer (Internalization) 17.5%
Direct Edge 9.8%
BATS 9.5%
Dark Pools 7.9%
Other Exchanges 3.7%
Other ECNs 1.0%

Electronic vs. Open Outcry

Bakos *et al.* [2000], opened a series of accounts at various full-service, discount and electronic securities brokers.

Their commissions for 100-share lots averaged $7.50 for electronic brokers and $47 for full-service voice brokers.

They found that full-service brokers were more likely to route orders to the principle exchanges than electronic brokers and that such orders were more likely to be improved.

However, for smaller orders, these price improvement advantages are more than offset by the higher brokerage commissions. Hence, specialists and market makers on exchanges were able to provide better order executions while brokers using electronic markets charged smaller commissions.

It appeared that smaller investors fared better with discount electronic brokers while larger transactions resulted in better after-commission executions on the principle exchanges.

C. Reasons for Fragmentation

- Fees
- Competition

- Innovation
- Long queues in constrained stocks

Fees

Exchanges charge an explicit fee for execution.

These include fees for trading the stock on the ASX, as well as clearing and settling.

As technology has made setting up exchanges cheaper, exchange fees have come down.

Most clearing/settling is done by a monopoly owner.

In 2010, ASIC gave Chi-X approval to enter Australian market. ASX reduced fees in response, as below.

Description	ASX Fee pre 1 July 2010	ASX Fee post 1 July 2010	Chi-X passive execution	Chi-X aggresive execution
Trade Execution Fee	0.280	0.150	0.06	0.12
Trade Execution — Auctions	0.280	0.280	—	—
On-market crossings	0.150	0.100	0.04	0.04
Off–market crossings	0.075	0.050	0.04	0.04

From trade to settlement

T Trade occurs

T+2 Shares and cash are "swapped"
Clearinghouse takes a fee

Exchange takes fee
for matching buyer
and seller

Clearing and settlement

The general *clearing* process involves two primary tasks: trade comparison (matching of trades) and settlement (delivery of securities or book entry).

Clearing refers to activities resulting in the settlement of claims of financial institutions against other financial institutions.

The operations department of a financial institution, often referred to as the institution's back office, is responsible for handling or overseeing the clearing and settlement processes.

A clearing firm is authorized by a clearing house to manage trade comparisons and other back office operations.

Leading clearing firms include Pershing, LLC, JP Morgan Clearing Corp. and National Financial Services, LLC.

A *clearing house* clears transactions for a market such as the NYSE. A clearing house facilitates the trade settlement between two clearing firms and seeks to ensure that the clearing firms honor their trade settlement obligations. The clearing house will typically guarantee the obligations of its member firms.

The clearing house steps into a transaction to be settled by its members and assumes the settlement obligations of both counterparties to the transaction, in effect becoming the counterparty to both sides of every transaction, a process known as *novation*. Thus, the clearing house, acting as a *central counterparty*, acts as the counterparty for each party to every transaction, and assumes all credit risk.

Competition

Until 2008, the TSX in Canada had a monopoly.

Until 2011 in Australia, the ASX held a monopoly over trading in Australia.

Monopolies have potential problems such as:

— High fees (monopoly rents)
— Lack of innovation

However, there are potential liquidity benefits from aggregating liquidity in one place > I know where to come if I want to trade.

Innovation

New markets bring new innovations with them.

Chi-X introduced new maker/taker pricing, faster trading engine and new order types.

IEX recently was accepted as an exchange in the US and has a speed bump to slow down high-frequency tradings (HFTs).

Long queues

The valuation of some stocks is easier than others.

Think of a bond it is very easy to value. This means prices do not change often.

This makes liquidity provision very valuable and leads to very long queues.

New markets create the option of a new queue.

Price/Time priority

Most modern markets allocate amongst limit orders based on price/time priority.

This means that I can get to the front of the queue by paying more.

If we all want to pay the same, it goes in order of when we arrived.

Fragmented markets do not need to observe time priority. Foucault and Menkveld [2008] show this is one of the benefits of fragmentation. This is like joining a shorter queue.

Other allocation mechanisms

Not all markets utilize price/time.

The LIFFE short-term interest rate future market in the UK changed from a pro-rata algorithm to time/pro-rata. This led to a significant change in how traders entered orders. Under pro-rata, time of entry does not matter, only size. In this environment very large orders were submitted. Under time/pro-rata both size and queue position were important. In the new system, traders would submit snake orders, with very large heads and small, long bodies.

What Makes a Good Competitor Exchange?

- Liquidity provision
- Market makers
- Liquidity begets liquidity
- Narrow spreads
- Low costs
- Large depth

How do we get people to trade?

HFT market makers (Like Virtu or Getco) are very necessary for a new market.

These traders may be sensitive to execution costs, so low prices are a good way.

Getco actually owned equity in Chi-X.

Some markets have adopted maker/taker rebates.

These rebates compensate liquidity provision, paid for by those who remove liquidity.

Liquidity Provision on Chi-X

Most liquidity is provided by Getco/Virtu.

Panel A: Liquidity Provision by Entrant ELPs

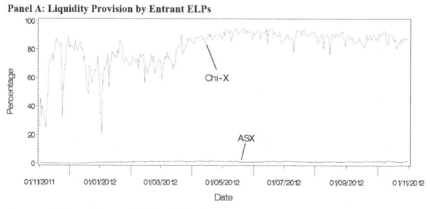

Source: Aitken, Chen and Foley [2016].

Impacts of Fragmentation

- Impacts for market quality
- Impacts for monopolies
- Impact for traders
- Additional complexity
- How to route orders smart order routers (SORs)

Impacts for market quality

There are network benefits to having all traders in one market, it makes it easy to find counterparties quickly.

Fragmentation can encourage competition between liquidity suppliers, leading to reduced spreads and increasing depth.

Foucault and Menkveld [2008] find that introducing competition in the Netherlands reduced explicit costs and increased depth due to competition between liquidity suppliers.

Aitken, Chen and Foley [2016] find a reduction in spreads for non-tick-constrained stocks and an increase in depth for tick-constrained stocks in Australia.

Impacts for monopolies

Monopolies may need to charge lower fees when competition enters (ASX reduced all fees which faced competition).

Competitors often bring innovation, e.g. ASX introduced dark order types, co-location and other innovative ideas.

In Canada, we have seen the use of inverted maker-taker and speed bumps to compete on order types.

Impact for traders

Fragmentation increases complexity.

However, it also comes with lower explicit and implicit costs.

These reductions can be very valuable for large traders.

More data feeds means more information processing, and potentially more costs.

Additional complexity

Numerous venues to deal with;
Each venue has their own separate order types;
Connections need to be made between the various venues;
Requires significant investments in infrastructure.

Routing orders

With multiple markets it becomes important to route to where best prices/depth exist. This is hard for an individual to do. To solve this, SORs are used.

These routers slice up orders across necessary markets.

Smart Order Router (SOR)

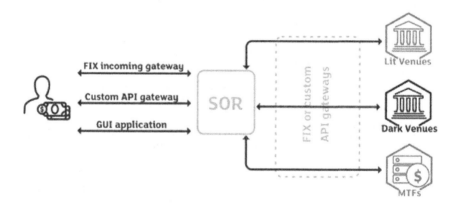

Problem with SOR: Quote Fade

Liquidity supply is fragmented across venues.

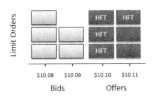  

Consequences of liquidity fade

The consequences of liquidity include the following features:

Liquidity supply is fragmented across venues;
Accessing this liquidity requires interacting with all venues;
HFT may be faster than regular traders;
Trader receives a fill on Bats, but orders are cancelled elsewhere.
Trader receives low fill rate;
Or trader is forced to pay more;
HFT can extract rents.

Solution: Speed bump

Trader can send order to IEX earlier, to ensure that both the LSE and IEX order arrive at the same time.
    This minimizes opportunity for HFT to remove liquidity.

RBC thor routing technology

Aims to protect order from being front-run;

— Aims to ensure all orders hit at same time.

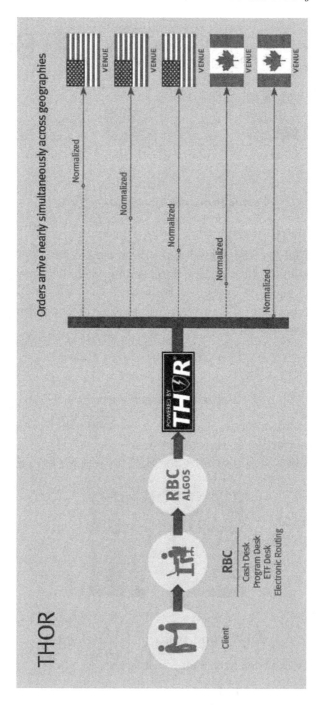

International fragmentation

Australia has 2 venues

Canada has 8

The US is highly fragmented and has around 45 venues!

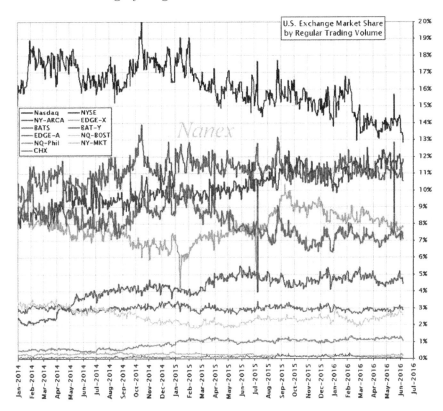

U.S. Exchange Market Share by Regular Trading Volume

D. Crossing Networks, Upstairs Markets and Dark Trading

Slippage, associated with large transactions, occurs when an order forces prices against the trader.

Crossing networks are ATSs that match buyers and sellers with agreed-upon quantities.

Crossing networks do not publicly display quotations, thereby enabling participants' anonymity.

Trades are priced by reference to prices obtained from other market. The crossing network then matches buy and sell orders at prices obtained from more traditional markets such as the NYSE.

This crossing procedure enables institutional traders to execute without exposing orders to competitors.

The crossing network, by having prices determined elsewhere, also prevents the price impact or pressure typically associated with auctions of large blocks of shares. Because crossing networks do not reveal prices or client identities, and that they represent non-displayed liquidity, they are sometimes referred to as *dark pools of liquidity*.

MidPoint Match and NASDAQ Crossing provide traders with opportunities to match orders anonymously at known benchmark (e.g. the midpoint of the spread) or closing or other prices several times a day.

The Securities and Exchange Commission [1998] defines crossing networks as systems that allow participants to enter unpriced orders to buy and sell securities. Orders are crossed at a specified time at a price derived from another market.

Dark Trading

- Dark vs. Lit Fragmentation
- What is dark trading?
- Dark pool price determination
- Types of dark trading
- Types of dark pools
- Internalization
- Dark pool pricing issues
- Impacts of dark trading

Dark vs. Lit fragmentation

Dark trading is an innovation which began around 2009.

Dark orders are hidden from the market.

Dark orders are priced dynamically from the best bid and ask typically at a price between the two.

For large orders, this can reduce their price impact.

If all trading were dark, this would remove all information from the limit order book, destroying price discovery.

Is Dark Trading Important? ASX $Bn/Trades

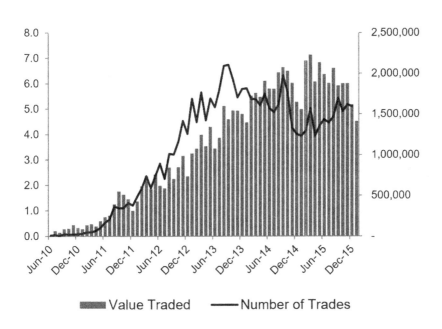

Why trade dark?

Dark trading helps to hide your order/trading intentions.

Also provides price improvement (typically) Alternatives?

Calling the street risky.

Put your order in the lit book (exposes intentions).

In 2005, ASX recorded broker IDs, large brokers complained they were being front run.

How Dark Trading Works

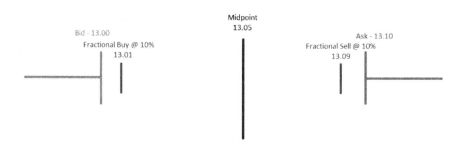

Different types of dark trading

Dark trades can be priced at the:

— Midpoint (13.05 in our previous figure)
— Fraction of the spread (13.01/13.09), this fraction can be basically 0% <fractional <50%
— Some pools in the US provide very small fractional improvements of 0.000001 cents
— NBBO that is 0% price improvement. This is not legal in Australia or Canada, but is common in Europe and the US.

Not all dark trading is equivalent

Two-sided vs. One-sided
   Three differences

1. Execution probabilities
2. Information revelation
3. Profitability of dark market making

Execution Probability for Impatient Orders

Balanced order flow subsidizes costs of executing unbalanced (e.g. inventory risk, adverse selection).

→ A smaller volume of balanced order flow, higher charge per unit of balanced order flow to cover costs of imbalance (Zhu, 2014);

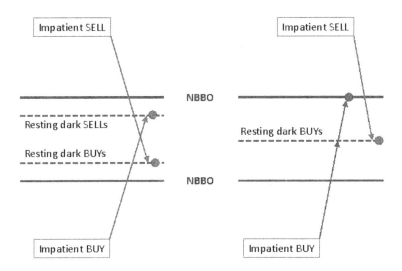

→ One-sided dark venue can increase lit spreads (Hendershott and Mendelson, 2000);

One-sided more harmful to liquidity than two-sided.

Information revelation

One-sided reveals dark order imbalance

→ provides information about trading intentions.

Profitability of dark market making

→ Dark market making can be profitable in two-sided dark markets (but not one-sided);
→ This encourages competition amongst lit market makers (Boulatov and George, 2015).

Is dark trading good or bad?

The short answer is, it depends on the type.

Recall there was two-sided (fractional) and one-sided (midpoint) dark liquidity.

Foley and Putnins [2016] show that two-sided liquidity benefits market quality, resulting in tighter spreads and increased informational efficiency.

The same benefits are not observed for one-sided dark trading.

E. Regulation

- Role of the regulator
- How to tell if the regulator is doing a good job
- Global regulatory bodies
- Recent regulatory developments

Mandate of regulators

Generally there are two components of a regulators job:

> Ensure markets are fair
> Ensure markets are efficient

But how can we evaluate fair and efficient?

Measuring the mandate

Efficiency is easier to measure, generally we want low transaction costs and prices which reflect fundamental value.

Transactions Costs Measures:

— Effective Spread
— Quoted Spread
— Price Impact
— Amihud Illiquidity
— Depth of the order book

Measuring efficiency

Price efficiency can be measured using things like:

> Volatility of prices (standard deviation)
> Adherence to a random walk (variance ratio)

Delay with which stocks incorporate index-level information
Autocorrelation of returns over fine intervals.

Measuring fair

Fairness is an ambiguous term. Generally fairness is interpreted as a
level playing field.

In reality, we can measure the extent to which participants engage
in prohibited conduct.

We could measure things such as:

Insider Trading
Closing price manipulation
Broker–client front-running
Spoofing
Pump and dump
Wash trading

Insider Trading

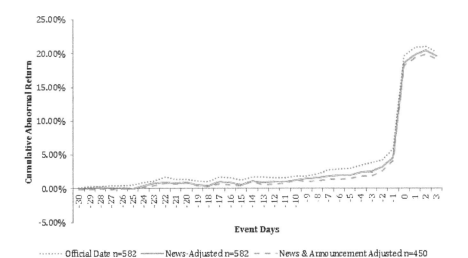

Closing Price Manipulation

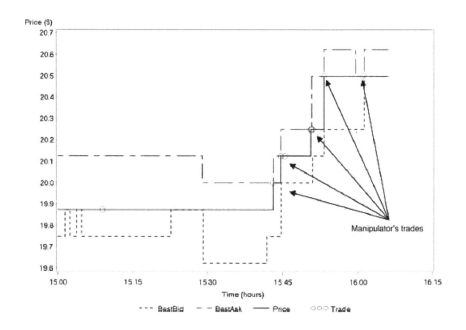

Closing Manipulation

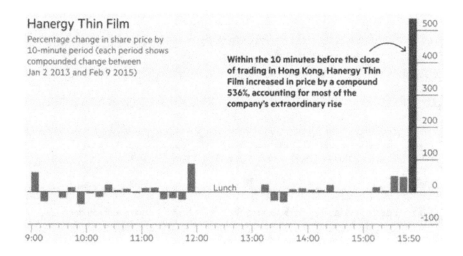

Broker–Client front-running

If I as a broker receive an order to buy $100 million worth of AMZN, I know this will increase the price.

If I was dishonest I could buy say $1 million for myself before I start the $100 million order.

Once the order was done, and pushed the price up, I would sell my stake for a profit. Obviously this is illegal and dishonest.

Spoofing

Features of spoofing include:

Entering lots of sell orders away from the best bid to give the appearance of selling pressure
Encouraging others to sell aggressively
Allowing you to buy cheaply;
Illegal.

Pump and dump

Buying lots of a small stock very slowly, then increasing the price and selling at a profit

Could increase the price by:

Releasing false positive information about the firm
Buying aggressively and hoping others jump on

Mostly works when there are falsely informed traders, or technical traders.

Wash trading

Trading with yourself for the purpose of inflating traded volume.
Sometimes associated with pump and dump schemes.

Global Regulatory Bodies

US: Securities Exchange Commission (SEC)
UK: Financial Conduct Authority (FCA)
Canada: Ontario Securities Commission

Australia: Australian Securities Exchange Commission (ASIC)
HK: Hong Kong Securities & Futures Commission
China: China Securities Regulatory Commission

Recent Regulatory Developments

- MiFID passporting in Europe
- Reg NMS trade through prohibition Best execution (Australia/ Europe)
- Minimum price improvement
- (Canada/Australia)

ADVERSE SELECTION AND MARKET MAKING

Summary of Lecture 5

A. Information and Trading

The *economics of information* is concerned with how information along with the quality and value of this information affect an economy and economic decisions. Information can be inexpensively created, can be reliable and, when reliable, is valuable.

The simplest microeconomics models assume that information is costless and all agents have equal access to relevant information.

Such assumptions do not hold in reality, and costly and asymmetric access to information very much affects how traders interact with each other.

Investors and traders look to the trading behavior of other investors and traders for information, which affects the trading behavior of informed investors who seek to limit the information that they reveal.

Here, we discuss the market mechanisms causing prices to react to the information content of trades (market impact or slippage), and how traders and dealers can react to this information content to maximize their own profits (or minimize losses).

This lecture is concerned primarily with problems that arise when traders and other market participants have inadequate, different (*asymmetric information availability*) and costly access to information.

Overview

- Costs for a market maker
- Role of informed traders
- Dynamics of the spread
- Measures of the spread
- Types of information
- Minimizing adverse selection

What is a Market Maker?

What does a Market Maker do?

Market makers fundamentally transfer liquidity through time.
This involves buying when people want to sell, and selling when people want to buy.
In return for this, market makers earn the spread, essentially buying low and selling high.
In early markets, this liquidity transfer could be across days, weeks or even months.

How Does a Market Maker Earn Money?

Market makers buy low and sell high.
This means they supply limit orders to buy passively at the bid, and sell passively at the ask.

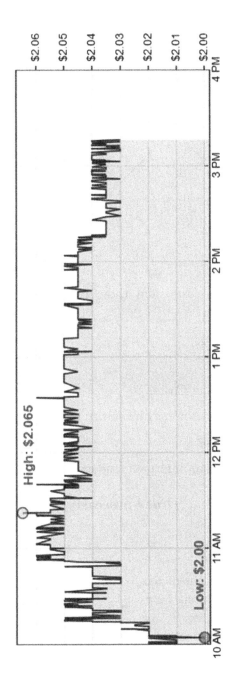

If prices bounce around between the bid and the ask they earn the spread.

Prices fluctuate between bid and ask

Market Making in Good Times

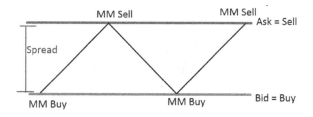

Costs for a market maker:

Market makers face costs, and these costs need to be recovered through the spread

- Order Processing

(e.g. exchange fees)

- Inventory Holding Costs

(costs of buying (and holding) inventory positions overnight)

- Adverse Selection

(cost of trading with an informed trader)

Order processing

Costs include:

— Exchange fees
— Clearing and settlement fees
— Financial transactions taxes
— Fees levied on orders
— Technology investment

— Connection fees

— Data fees

Inventory holding costs

These costs develop as market makers deal with inventory risk.

Holding stocks (long or short) exposes the market maker to changes in fundamental value.

Essentially, the market maker is becoming an investor.

Adverse Selection

Adverse selection refers to pre-contractual opportunism where one contracting party uses his private information to the other counterparty's disadvantage.

For example, the adverse selection problem can arise when a pyromaniac purchases fire insurance.

The agent (insured or customer) has private information with respect to the higher anticipated costs of the insurance coverage or lease, but pays a pooling premium for the incident or casualty coverage.

This private information affects the behavior or insurers and other insured clients, in what might otherwise be taken to be a suboptimal manner, referred to as the adverse selection problem.

In a financial trading context, adverse selection occurs when one trader with secret or special information uses that information to her advantage at the expense of her counterparty in trade.

Trade counterparties realize that they might fall victim to adverse selection, so they carefully monitor trading activity in an effort to discern which trades are likely to reflect special information.

For example, large or numerous buy (sell) orders originating from the same trader are likely to be perceived as being motivated by special information. Trade counterparties are likely to react by adjusting their offers (bids) upwards (downwards), resulting in slippage.

Adverse Selection

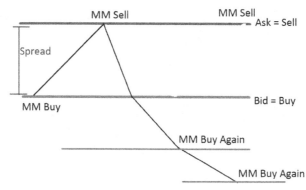

Adverse Selection in Dealer Markets

Bagehot [1971] described a market where dealers or market makers stand by to provide liquidity to every trader who wishes to trade, losing on trades with informed traders but recovering these losses by trading with uninformed, noise or liquidity-motivated traders.

The market maker sets prices and trades to ensure this outcome, on average.

The market maker merely recovers his operating costs along with a "normal return".

In this framework, trading is a zero sum or neutral game; uninformed investors will lose more than they make to informed traders.

Market makers observe buying and selling pressure on prices, set prices accordingly, often making surprisingly little use of fundamental analysis when making their pricing decisions.

The theoretical model of Kyle [1985] describes the trading behavior of informed traders and uninformed market makers in an environment with noise traders.

Informed Traders

Informed traders are necessary to ensure prices are efficient.

These traders may do research to decide if a stock is undervalued or overvalued, or possess some special kind of knowledge.

These traders profit by trading on their information.

If they are more informed than the market maker, these traders will always win on average.

Informed traders want to make the most they can from their information.

Trading fast and above average volume is in their advantage, which may push prices up.

If they trade too slowly, they will not make enough profit to cover the costs of information.

This trading will depend on how many other traders there are, the value of the information, and the time of revelation of the information.

Cost Recovery

Market makers need to recover the costs of liquidity provision from their customers.

They do this by changing the size of the spread.

Since they will always lose to informed traders, they need to profit from the uninformed.

This profit needs to (at least) cover all the costs of liquidity provision.

Components of the Spread

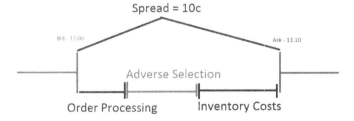

Uninformed Traders

- Trade based on information that is already reflected in prices are incorrect.

- Their trades **are not correlated** with the fundamental value of the security.

The role of uninformed traders

- Since market makers (MMs) lose to informed traders, they must profit from uninformed traders.
- This profit must be at least as great as the loss.

Market Makers Job

MM observes (unbalanced) total order flow $(X)X = $ informed$(i) + $ Uninformed (U).

If I receive more buys than sells, adjust quotes up. If receive more sells than buys, adjust quotes down.

How much I adjust quotes depends on the composition of informed vs. uninformed.

Given discrete time periods, MMs need to set the price at which they will balance X.

Kyles Lambda

$$\lambda = \sqrt{\frac{1}{4}\frac{\Sigma_0}{\sigma_u^2}} = \frac{1}{2}\sqrt{\frac{\Sigma_0}{\sigma_u^2}}.$$

- λ is the dealer price adjustment for total stock demand or *the illiquidity adjustment*;
- Σ_0 is informed trader private information;
- σ_u^2 is the level of noise trading;
- The dealer price adjustment is proportional to the square root of this ratio, increasing as private information Σ_0 is increasing and decreasing as noise trading increases.
- If private information is very valuable (i.e. lots of information asymmetry — think small mining stocks), then the adjustment will be very large.
- If there is lots of noise trading, then order flow is less informative, and the adjustment will be much smaller.
- Basically this is a reflection of the "signal to noise" ratio.

Measurements of Spread

- Quoted Spread
- Effective Spread
- Realized Spread
- Price Impact

$10.08 $10.10	$10.20 $10.25
Bids	Offers

$$Ask - Bid$$

Quoted spread

- Quoted spread measures the difference between the best bid and best ask.
- Here it is $10.20 - 10.10 = 10c$.
- It represents what the liquidity suppliers demand on average to cover their costs.
- We often time-weight this spread across the day.

$10.00 $10.10	$10.20 $10.25
Bids	Offers

$$Direction * (Price - Midpoint) * 2$$

Effective spread

- Effective spread measures the price paid by liquidity demanders — when they access liquidity
- Direction is 1 for buys and -1 for sells
- Imagine trade which buys 100 shares at 10.20
- ES $= 1 \times (10.20 - 10.15) \times 2 = 10c$
- Imagine trade which sells 200 shares: 100 at 10.10 and 100 at 10.00
- ES $= -1 \times (10.05 - 10.15) \times 2 = 20c$
- This trader demanded more shares, and so paid a higher overall cost

- It represents what the liquidity demanders *actually* paid
- We often weigh these by volume traded in a day.

Effective spread components

- Effective spread is composed of two components — temporary and permanent
- Trades can cause temporary imbalance of supply and demand — this will revert in a small period of time
- Liquidity suppliers profit from these temporary imbalances. We call this realized spread
- (Informed) trades can also reveal information, causing prices to move permanently
- We refer to this as the Price Impact (or Adverse Selection).

$$Direction * (Price - Midpoint_{t+5}) * 2$$

$10.00 $10.10		$10.20 $10.25
Bids	Trade	Offers

$10.00 $10.12		$10.22 $10.25
Bids	Trade + 5m	Offers

Realized spread

- Realized spread measures the return to liquidity suppliers (i.e. MMs)
- It measures how much the liquidity supplier makes, assuming they unwind their position some time later (say 5 minutes)
- Imagine trade which buys 100 shares at 10.20
- Five minutes later midpoint has increased by 2c to 10.17
- RS = $1 \times (10.20 - 10.17) \times 2 = 6c$
- This liquidity supplier did not earn the whole spread because the price increased after they sold
- We often weigh these by volume traded in a day.

$$Direction * (Midpoint_{t+5} - Midpoint) * 2$$

$10.00 $10.10		$10.20 $10.25
Bids	Trade	Offers

$10.00		$10.22 $10.25
Bids	Trade + 5m	Offers

Price impact

- Price Impact measures the permanent increase in price due to a trade
- It measures how much a trader has in the market some time later (say 5 minutes)
- Imagine trade which buys 100 shares at 10.20
- Five minutes later midpoint has increased by 2c to 10.17
- PI $= 1 \times (10.17 - 10.15) \times 2 = 4c$
- This liquidity supplier did not earn the whole spread because the price increased against them after they sold
- Effective spread = Realized spread + Price Impact
- 10c = 6c + 4c.

Types of Information

- Fundamental Information
- Insider Information
- Order Flow Information
- Statistical Information

Fundamental information

- For prices to be efficient they must reflect all available public information.
- This information is costly to gather, process and turn into useful price data.
- Those who do process this data can profit, however, by trading.
- This trading impounds the information into prices, ensuring that they stay "rational".

- This is primarily done by investment managers and investment banks. These traders can be considered "informed".

Inside information

- Insiders know private information.
- It is illegal for them to trade on this information.
- However, if they do, they will always "win" since they know things the market does not.
- These traders will encourage VERY efficient prices.
- These traders will also cause lots of adverse selection for market makers.

Order flow information

- In today's high frequency markets, large orders are typically broken up into small orders across the day.
- These are known as volume-weighted average price (VWAP) or time-weighted average price (TWAP) execution strategies.
- These strategies leave footprints that traders can identify.
- Large orders are likely to push prices in the same direction (up for buys, down for sells).
- This means that market makers need to be careful of trading with large traders, as they will impose adverse selection too.

Theory

Kyles [1985] theoretical model and complementary models discussed in the following provide the important lessons:

- Understanding the implications for markets of having both informed and uninformed traders;
- Understanding how market makers update their quotes.

B. Noise Traders

Noise traders trade on the basis of what they falsely believe to be special information or misinterpret useful information.

Noise traders make investment and trading decisions based on incorrect perceptions or analyses. Do noise traders distort prices? Maybe yes if:

- noise traders trade in large numbers
- their trading behavior is correlated
- their effects cannot be mitigated by informed and rational traders.

Milton Friedman suggested that traders who produce positive profits do so by trading against less rational or poorly informed investors who tend to move prices away from their fundamental or correct values.

Fama argued that when irrational trading does occur, security prices will not be significantly affected because sophisticated traders will react quickly to exploit and eliminate deviations from fundamental economic values.

Figlewski [1979] suggested that it might take irrational investors a long time to lose their money and for prices to reflect security intrinsic values, but they are doomed in the long run.

Noise traders might be useful, perhaps even necessary for markets to function. Without noise traders, markets would be informationally efficient and maybe no one would want to trade. Even with asymmetric information access, informed traders can fully reveal their superior information through their trading activities, and prices would reflect this information and ultimately eliminate the motivation for information-based trading.

That is, as Black [1986] argued, without noise traders, dealers would widen their spreads to avoid losing profits to informed traders such that no trades would ever be executed. However, noise traders do impose on other traders the risk that prices might move irrationally. This risk imposed by noise traders might discourage arbitrageurs from acting to exploit price deviations from fundamental values. Prices can deviate significantly from rational valuations, and can remain different for long periods. Arbitrageurs might ask themselves the following question: Does my ability to remain solvent exceed the asset prices ability to remain irrational?

Kyle [1985]: Informed Traders, Market Makers and Noise Traders

Suppose two rational traders have access to the same information and are otherwise identical. They have no motivation to trade.

Now, suppose they have different information. Will they trade? Not if one trader believes that the other will trade only if the other has information that will enable him to profit in the trade at the first trader's expense.

Rational traders will not trade against other rational traders even if their information differs. This is a variation of the Akerlof Lemon Problem.

So, why do we observe so much trading in the marketplace? Most of us believe that others are not as informed or rational as we are or that others do not have the same ability to access and process information that we do.

Kyle examines trading and price setting in a market where some traders are informed and others (noise or liquidity traders) are not.

Dealers or market makers serve as intermediaries between informed and uninformed traders.

Dealers set security prices that enable them to survive even without the special information enjoyed by informed traders.

Kyle models how informed traders use their information to maximize their trading profits given that their trades yield useful information to market makers.

Furthermore, market makers will learn from the informed traders trading, and the informed trader's trading activity will seek to disguise his special information from the dealer and noise traders.

Illustration: Kyle's Adverse Selection Model

Sourced from Teall [2012] pp. 125–126

- Suppose that the unconditional value of a stock in a Kyle framework is normally distributed with an expected value equal to $E[v] = \$50$ and a variance equal to $\Sigma_0 = 30$.

- An informed trader has private information that the value of the stock is actually $v = \$45$ per share.
- Uninformed investor trading is random and normally distributed with an expected net share demand of zero σ_u^2 equal to 5,000.
- The dealer can observe the total level of order volume $X = x + u$, where u reflects noise trader transactions and x reflects informed demand, but the dealer cannot distinguish between x and u.
- The ability of the informed trader to camouflage his activity is directly related to σ_u^2 and inversely related to x.
- What would be the level of informed trader demand for the stock? We solve for x as follows, using the following equation:

$$x = -\frac{E[v]}{\sqrt{\frac{\sum_0}{\sigma_u^2}}} + \frac{\nu}{\sqrt{\frac{\sum_0}{\sigma_u^2}}} = -\frac{50}{\sqrt{\frac{30}{5,000}}}$$

$$+\frac{45}{\sqrt{\frac{30}{5,000}}} = \frac{-5}{0.07746} = -64.5497$$

Informed demand and dealer pricing coefficients

- The informed trader would wish to sell an infinite number of shares to earn a \$5 profit on each, but cannot because the dealer would correctly infer that his share sales convey meaningful information, and the dealer's price revisions would lead to slippage.
- Thus, at what level does the dealer set his price, given the total demand $X = [x + u] = -64.5497 + 0$ that he observes? First, we solve for parameters in the dealer pricing equation:

$$\alpha = -\frac{E[\nu]}{\sqrt{\frac{\sum_0}{\sigma_u^2}}} = -\frac{50}{\sqrt{\frac{30}{5,000}}} = -645.49$$

$$\beta = \frac{1}{\sqrt{\frac{\sum_0}{\sigma_u^2}}} = \frac{1}{\sqrt{\frac{30}{5,000}}} = 12.91$$

$$\lambda = \frac{1}{2}\sqrt{\frac{\sum_0}{\sigma_u^2}} = \frac{1}{2}\sqrt{\frac{60}{10,000}} = 0.0387$$

The Dealer Price

The dealer sets the price as follows:

$$p = E[\nu] + \left[\frac{\beta \sum_0}{\beta^2 \sum_0 + \sigma_u^2}\right] [x + u - \alpha - \beta E[\nu]]$$

$$= 50 + \left[\frac{12.91 \cdot 30}{12.91^2 \cdot 30 + 5,000}\right] [-64.5497 + 0 + 645.49 - 12.91 \cdot 50]$$

$$= 50 - 0.0387 \cdot 64.5497 = 47.50$$

C. Adverse Selection and the Spread

Walrasian markets assume perfect and frictionless competition and symmetric information availability.

In security markets, imperfect competition, bid-offer imbalances and frictions often reveal themselves in bid-offer spreads. Here, we are concerned with the determinants of the bid-offer spread. The evolution of prices through time should provide insight as to what affects the spread.

If market frictions were the only factors affecting the spread, we should expect that, in the absence of new information, execution prices would tend to bounce between bid and ask prices. Thus, frictions such as transactions costs will tend to either leave execution prices unchanged or change in the opposite direction. Thus, transactions costs tend to induce negative serial correlation in asset prices.

- Asymmetric information produces positive serial correlation in asset prices. Suppose that asymmetric information is the only source of the spread, such that transaction prices reflect information communicated by transactions. Transactions executed at bid prices would cause permanent drops in prices to reflect negative information and transactions executed at offer prices would cause permanent increases in prices to reflect positive information. If price changes are solely a function of random news arrival, price changes will be random. If the distribution of information is asymmetric, prices will exhibit positive serial correlation as informed traders communicate their information through their trading activity (recall that this is what informed traders try to avoid in the Kyle model). Thus, the extent to which information distribution is asymmetric will affect the serial correlation of asset prices.

- Inventory costs (such as unsystematic risk from the dealers inability to diversify) will tend to cause negative serial correlations in price quotes. Transactions at the bid will tend to cause risk-averse dealers to reduce their bid quotes as they become more reluctant not to over-diversify their inventories. Similarly, transactions at the ask will tend to cause dealers to raise their quotes as they become more reluctant not to under-diversify their inventories.
- Inventory costs and transactions costs will tend to lead towards negative serial correlation in security prices.
- Asymmetric information availability will lead toward positive serial correlation in security prices as transactions communicate new information.

The Demsetz [1968] Immediacy Argument

Order imbalances impose waits on impatient traders requiring immediacy.

The costs of providing immediacy to liquidity traders include order processing costs (transactions costs), information and adverse selection costs, inventory holding costs, costs of absorbing inventory risks and costs of providing trading options.

The bid-offer spread provides the dealer compensation for assuming these costs on behalf of the market.

In the Demsetz [1968] analysis, buyers and sellers of a security are each of two types, one of which who wants an immediate transaction and a second who wants a transaction, but can wait.

Buy and sell orders arrive to the market in a non-synchronous fashion, causing order imbalances.

An imbalance of traders demanding an immediate trade forces the price to move against themselves, causing less patient traders to pay for immediacy. The greater the costs of trading, and the greater the desire for immediacy, the greater will be the market spread.

Glosten and Milgrom [1985] Information Asymmetry Model

- The Glosten and Milgrom [1985] adverse selection model assumes that dealer spreads are based on the likelihood π that an informed trader will trade.
- Trades arrive to the market maker, each with some random chance of originating from either an informed or uninformed trader.
- The asset can take on one of two prices, a high price P_H and a low price P_L, each with probability $1/2$.
- Uninformed traders will not pay more than P_H for the asset and they will not sell for less than P_L.
- Risk neutral liquidity traders value the asset at $(P_H + P_L)/2$.
- When setting his quotes, the dealer needs to account for the probability that an informed trader will transact at his quote, and will set his bid price P_b and ask price P_a as follows:

$$P_b = \pi P_L + (1 - \pi)(P_H + P_L)/2,$$
$$P_a = \pi P_H + (1 - \pi)(P_H + P_L)/2.$$

- The spread is simply the difference between the ask and bid prices:

$$P_a - P_b = \pi(P_H - P_L).$$

- Thus, in the single-period Glosten and Milgrom model, the spread is a function of the likelihood that there exists an informed trader in the market and the uncertainty in the value of the traded asset.
- The greater the uncertainty in the value of the traded asset as reflected by $(P_H + P_L)/2$, and the greater the probability π that a trade has originated with an informed trader, the greater will be the spread.

Other Relevant Models and their Assumptions

The Stoll [1978] Inventory Model

A dealer needs to maintain inventories in assets in which he makes a market to sell to investors as well as cash to purchase assets from investors. Suppose that a dealer currently without inventory in a particular asset trades so as to maximize his expected utility level.

The inventory model assumes that the dealer's wealth level could be subject to some uncertain normally distributed security return r whose expected value is zero and variance.

The Copeland and Galai [1983] Options Model

A bid provides prospective sellers a put on the asset, with the exercise price of the put equal to the bid.

An offer provides a call to other traders. Thus, when the dealer posts both bid and offer quotes, the spread is, in effect, a short *strangle* provided to the market. Both legs of this strangle are more valuable when the risk of the underlying security is higher.

An options pricing model can be used to value this dealer spread. Ultimately, this "implied premium" associated with this dealer spread is paid by liquidity traders who trade without information.

Informed traders make money at the expense of the dealer, who ultimately earns it back at the expense of the uninformed trader.

The Copeland and Galai model, as presented here, does not have a mechanism to allow trading activity to convey information from informed traders to dealers and uninformed traders. Nonetheless, in the Copeland and Galai option-based model, the spread widens as the uncertainty with respect to the security price increases.

LECTURE 6

BEHAVIORAL FINANCE

Summary of Lecture 6

A. Rational Investor Paradigms

- Many financial models assume that all investors and all corporate managers are rational individuals who prefer more wealth to less and seek to maximize their wealth.
- Behavioral finance is concerned with the actual behavior and thinking of individuals who make financial decisions.

This chapter explores how investors and traders (as well as all human beings) are impacted by behavioral biases "hard-wired" in their mind using a set of examples that explain common concepts in behavioral finance such as prospect theory, anchoring, overconfidence and sensation seeking. Strategies for dealing with these biases so that they do not affect decisions adversely are discussed.

The St. Petersburg Paradox and the Expected Utility Paradigm

- In 1713, Nicholas Bernoulli reasoned that a rational gambler should be willing to buy a gamble for its expected value. His cousin, Daniel Bernoulli, presented his paradigm in 1738 at a conference of mathematicians in St. Petersburg.
- His extended problem, commonly referred to as the St. Petersburg Paradox, was concerned with why gamblers would pay only a finite sum for a gamble with an infinite expected value.

- Suppose, in Bernoulli's paradigm, the coin lands on its head on the first toss, the gamble payoff is \$2. If the coin lands tails, it is tossed again. If the coin lands heads on this second toss, the payoff is \$4, otherwise, it is tossed a third time. The process continues until the payoff is determined by the coin finally landing heads. Where n equals infinity, the expected value of this gamble is determined by the following:

$$E[V] = (0.5^1 \times 2^1) + (0.5^2 \times 2^2) + (0.5^3 \times 2^3) + \ldots + (0.5^\infty \times 2^\infty)$$

- The payoff 2^n is realized with probability equal to 0.5^n. The expected value of the gamble equals the sum of all potential payoffs times their associated probabilities:

$$E[V] = (0.5^1 \times 2^1) + (0.5^2 \times 2^2) + (0.5^3 \times 2^3) + \ldots + (0.5^n \times 2^n)$$
$$E[V] = (0.5 \times 2) + (0.5 \times 2) + (0.5 \times 2) + \ldots + (0.5 \times 2)$$
$$E[V] = (1) + (1) + (1) + \ldots + (1)$$

- Since there is some possibility that the coin is tossed tails an infinity of times ($n = \infty$), the expected or actuarial value of this gamble is infinite.
- Paradoxically, Bernoulli found that none of the esteemed mathematicians at the conference would be willing to pay an infinite sum (or, in most cases, even a large sum) of money for the gamble with infinite actuarial value.
- Bernoulli opined that the resolution to this paradox is the now commonly accepted notion of "diminishing marginal utility."

Utility of Wealth Von Neuman and Morgenstern: Axioms of Choice

B. Prospect Theory

- **Losses and Inconsistency**
  Consider the following example choice of gambles:
- **Gamble A:** 0.33 probability of receiving 2,500, 0.66 of receiving 2,400 and 0.01 of receiving 0
- **Gamble B:** 100% probability of receiving 2,400

Kahneman and Tversky found that 82% of their experiment participants preferred Gamble B to Gamble A. However, they offered the same set of participants the following second set of gambles:

- **Gamble A*:** 0.33 probability of receiving 2,500, 0.67 of receiving 0
- **Gamble B*:** 0.34 probability of receiving 2,400 and 0.66 of receiving 0

In the second part of this experiment, 83% of participants preferred Gamble A* to B*.

Frames Versus Substance

Consider the following example when individuals are asked from two different perspectives to select from radiation or surgery for cancer treatment:

Survival Frame

- Surgery: Of 100 people having surgery, 90 live through the postoperative period, 68 are alive at the end of the first year, and 34 are alive at the end of 5 years.
- Radiation: Of 100 people having radiation therapy, all live through the treatment, 77 are alive at the end of the first year, and 22 are alive at the end of 5 years.

Mortality Frame

- Surgery: Of 100 people having surgery, 10 die during surgery or the postoperative period, 32 die by the end of the first year, and 66 die by the end of 5 years.
- Radiation: Of 100 people having radiation therapy, none die during treatment, 23 die by the end of the first year, and 78 die by the end of 5 years.

  Although the information presented in the "Survival Frame" is identical to that presented in the "Mortality Frame", 18% of respondents preferred radiation therapy when presented with the "Survival Frame" compared with 44% when presented with the "Mortality Frame."

Maintaining the Status Quo: Joe and his Opera Tickets

The following story was taken from the Wall Street Journal:

On the way to the opera, Joe loses his pair of $50 tickets. Most likely, he will not buy another pair — spending [a total of] $200 [including $100 on the lost tickets] to hear "La Boheme" seems a bit much. But suppose, instead, he arrives at the theater tickets-in-hand, but discovers he has lost a $100 bill. He could sell his tickets, which would net him the same result as in the first case — out $100 and out the tickets. But he probably won't sell. ... Joe may think he is entirely rational, but he leans consistently toward the status quo.

- This particular type of bias to maintain the *status quo* is sometimes referred to as the endowment effect.
- This effect causes losses or what is given up to weight more heavily in the decision-making process than gains or what is acquired.
- This effect seems to manifest itself in investing through a seeming reluctance to sell stocks, particularly stocks that have lost value.
- Numerous studies have documented investors' reluctance to sell their "losers" to capture their tax write-offs. The tax write-off implications of selling a stock that has lost value are enhanced when "losers" are sold before year's end.
- Some observers refer to this phenomenon as "fear of regret."
- More generally, studies have suggested that this endowment effect or disposition effect might lead stock markets to underreact to news and exacerbate momentum effects in stock prices.

Anchoring

- Anchoring is where the decision maker places undue emphasis on some factor, number or measure.
- Kahneman and Tversky asked participants in an experiment to spin a roulette wheel with numbers from 1 to 100 and then estimate the number of countries in Africa. They found that participants' estimates were unduly influenced by the result of the roulette wheel spin result. Low roulette wheel outcomes were followed by lower estimates of the numbers of African countries.

- Similarly, Genesove and Mayer [2001] found that sellers of houses and apartments tend to be unduly influenced by purchase prices of their homes.
- There is similar evidence suggesting that investors may be unduly biased by purchase prices of their securities. Studies have found that amateur traders are more affected by endowment and anchoring effects than professionals.

C. Behavioral Finance

- Behavioral finance, largely rooted in Prospect Theory, is concerned with the impact of human emotions and cognitive impairments on investment decision making.

The Monty Hall Judgment Error

- Consider a scenario based on the late 1960's game show "Let's Make a Deal."
- Monty Hall would offer contestants an opportunity to choose one prize hidden behind one of the three identical doors.
- Prizes hidden behind two of the three doors were worthless (if the contestant selected either of these doors, he was "zonked,"), but the prize hidden behind the third was valuable.
- The contestant would choose the door behind his prize was to be hidden.
- Before allowing the contestant to see whether she had won the valuable prize, and with increasing audience anticipation, Mr. Hall would then typically show the contestant the worthless prize behind one of the two doors that the contestant did not select.
- He would then offer the contestant an opportunity to switch her selection to the prize behind the third door.
- The contestant's problem is whether to stick with her original selection or to switch her selection to the prize hidden behind the third door.
- Regardless of what prize remains behind the first door selected by the contestant, Mr. Hall will reveal the worthless prize behind a

second door. Hence, the probability of a valuable prize behind the first door remains $1/3$.

- We know that Mr. Hall will not reveal the prize behind the selected door, so its probability of being the desirable prize is unchanged.
- The door that Mr. Hall will select to open will have a worthless prize with probability one.
- What is the probability that the valuable prize is behind the third door? This probability must be $1 - 1/3 - 0 = 2/3$.
- Why? Remember that Mr. Hall will not open a second door with a valuable prize behind it. This doubles the probability that the valuable prize is behind the third door.
- Hence, the contestant should always switch his selection to maximize his probability of obtaining the valuable prize. Most contestants did not.
- Most people have no difficulty estimating that the initial probability of $1/3$ for the prize behind any one of the three doors. This heuristic has served most people well for years. However, people tend to use the same heuristic when a "zonk" is revealed behind one of the doors, leading them to conclude that there is a 50/50 probability that the prize is behind one of them. This heuristic is difficult to abandon when the nature of the problem changed, as the problem solution shifts from an unconditional probability to a less intuitive conditional probability.
- Perhaps, more interestingly, most subjects refuse to accept the validity of mathematical proofs offered to demonstrate the wisdom of switching doors.
- Furthermore, most subjects continue to refuse to switch doors after being permitted to watch repeated trials of this experiment where the third door leads to the valuable prize with a frequency of approximately $2/3$.

The Monte Hall Problem and Markets

- Kluger and Wyatt [2004] conducted experiments to determine how a market might behave in such a scenario.
- Kluger and Wyatt gathered subjects in a laboratory setting and had them compete to select investments, whose payoffs were

"behind doors." "Investors" participated in repeated trials, were offered opportunities to select doors and then compete to pay to either retain or switch their selections.

- Investors consistently mispriced the investments.
- However, when as few as two "rational investors" who correctly estimated the probabilities were included in the trials, prices to switch were roughly double the prices to retain original selections.
- Hence, it seemed that competition between only two rational investors out of many were necessary for market prices to reflect rational probabilities.

Dumb, dumber and dead

- There have been many cases of strong correlations between stocks with similar ticker symbols.
- Massmutual Corporate Investors (ticker: MCI) a NYSE listed fund was strongly correlated with those of MCI Communications (ticker: MCIC)
  - Massmutual's returns were far more correlated with MCI's than AT&T or any of the other telecommunications firms were.
  - It seems that investors bought shares of Massmutual and held them for long periods of time, believing that they had invested in MCI.
- The Castle Convertible Fund has been confused with the Czech Value Fund (CVF). Castle (ticker: CVF).
- Early exercises of CBOE call options seem to be irrational, where customers of both full-service and discount brokers seem to exhibit irrational exercise behavior, while traders in large investment houses did not.
- Perhaps the most notorious of under-performing funds during the 1990's bull market was the Steadman Technology & Growth Fund.
  - Its returns during part of this decade were −5% in 1992, −8% in 1993, −37% in 1994, −28% in 1995, −30% in 1996 and −28% in 1997. Market returns were positive in each of these years.
  - Portfolio turnover rates and transactions costs were extremely high, expense ratios were frequently in the 6–7% range, and

Steadman seemed not to have a coherent investment strategy, indiscriminately investing in stocks and other securities.

- The SEC forced the fund to stop accepting money from new investors in 1989.
- When the Technology & Growth Fund was finally shut down, about 30% of the redemption checks were returned, presumably because the shareholders were dead.

Overconfidence

- How many investors believe that they are better than average traders? How many drivers think that they are better than average? How many people think that they are dumb (less intelligent than average)?
- *Good decision making requires more than knowledge of facts, concepts and relationships, it also requires metaknowledge — an understanding of the limits of our knowledge. Unfortunately, we tend to have a deeply rooted overconfidence in our beliefs and judgments.*
- To test for overconfidence and compare results across professions, Russo and Schoemaker created and administered a 10-question test similar to one we will examine shortly.
- Before discussing the results of their study, take the test yourself.
- Since you will probably not know the exact answers for each of these questions, your objective is to guess by setting minimum and maximum bounds for each of the questions such that you are 80% confident that the actual answer will be within the 80% confidence interval that you set.
- Obviously, if your range is from 0 to infinity for each question, the correct answers will all fall within your confidence intervals. But, again, your goal is to answer only with 80% certainty, so narrow your ranges accordingly.

Overconfidence Test

Overconfidence and trading

- Several studies show that trading activity increases when traders are overconfident. Overconfident traders underreact to the information content of trades by rational traders, causing positive serial correlation in returns.

- Barber and Odean, in studies of trading in 10,000 and over 60,000 discount-brokerage accounts from 1987 to 1993 and from 1991 to 1996, found that trading by investors reduced their levels of wealth below what they would have realized with buy-and-hold strategies.
- A year after the trades, the average investor ended up over 9% worse off than if had he done nothing.
- In another study of 1,607 investors, Barber and Odean [2002] found that investors that had switched from phone-based trading to Internet systems increased their portfolio turnover rates from 70% per year to 120%. They outperformed the market on average by 2.35% before switching and were outperformed by the market by 3.5% after switching.
- Amateur traders clearly underperformed the market and the most active traders experienced the worst performance.
- Interestingly, investors who traded the least actually beat market indices.
- There is evidence that professional stock analysts who have outperformed their peers in the recent past tend to become overconfident and underperform their peers in subsequent periods.
- People tend to be overconfident in their own judgments and experts tend to be more prone to overconfidence than novices and maintain reputations for their expertise.
- However, there is an upside to overconfidence. Overconfidence may lead "to higher motivation, greater persistence, more effective performance and ultimately more success."
- The more aggressive trading behavior of overconfident professional traders help them to generate higher profits than their more rational competitors.

Overconfidence, Gender, Entertainment and Testosterone

- Men seem more prone to overconfidence than women, particularly in male-dominated realms such as finance.

- Barber and Odean [2001] find that men trade 45% more frequently than women, reducing their returns relative to market indices by 2.65% compared to 1.72% for women.
- Differences between men and women in the trading realm are so striking that one might ask whether people trade for entertainment in addition to wealth creation.
- Evolutionary biologists have argued that males of many species tend to take more risks than their female counterparts. They suggest that males take increased risks to enhance their status in order to create more opportunities to reproduce, knowing that prospective mates prefer higher-status males.
- Testosterone and cortisol, hormones more abundant in the male body than in the female, have clear cognitive and behavioral effects.

  - Testosterone is more prevalent in the bodies of winning male athletes than in losing athletes
  - Cortisol is known to increase in situations characterized by uncontrollability, novelty, and uncertainty

- Coates and Herbert [2008] sampled, under real working conditions, endogenous steroids from a group of male London traders in the City of London.

  - A trader's morning testosterone level predicts his day's trading profitability. More specifically, they found that on mornings when testosterone levels were high, 14 of the 17 traders in their study realized higher trading profits.
  - They also found that a trader's cortisol rises with both the variance of his trading results and the volatility of the market. Thus, higher testosterone levels seem to contribute to trading returns while cortisol levels increased as risk and risk-taking increase.
  - Chronically elevated testosterone levels could have negative effects on returns because testosterone has also been found to lead to impulsivity and sensation seeking and to harmful risk taking.

- If individual traders, particularly aggressive individual traders lose money relative to the market, who makes money? Consider a study by Barber *et al.* [2007] covering the entire Taiwanese stock market from 1995 to 1999. They document that individual investor trading results in consistently large losses averaging approximately 3.8%. These losses are attributable to aggressive trading behavior. On the other hand, institutional investors outperform the market by 1.5% (after commissions and taxes, but before other costs). Both aggressive and passive trades of institutions are profitable. Perhaps, aggressive trading behavior leads to wealth transfers from amateurs to professional traders.

Sensation-seeking, Investor Moods, the Weather and Investment Returns

- Aggressive trading behavior does seem related to overconfidence, but there is also a good reason to think that it can be related to sensation or thrill seeking, just as gambling might be. In fact, research suggest that aggressive trading is directly related to the number of speeding tickets that traders receive.
- There is some evidence that investors' moods might significantly affect market performance.

  - Seasonal Disorder, medical condition where the shorter days in fall and winter lead to depression for many people, is associated with reduced stock market returns after adjusting for a variety of other factors.
  - Stock market returns are higher during the spring quarter than during the fall quarter.
  - Northern and southern hemisphere returns seem 6 months out of phase.

- Several studies have found that weather might affect market returns.
- Cloud cover in the city of a country's major stock exchange is negatively correlated with daily stock index returns.
- Stock market performance was simply worse on cloudy days. In New York City, there was a 24.8% annualized return for all days forecast to be perfectly sunny, and an 8.7% average return occurred on cloudy days.

- However, another study found that cloudy days were associated with wider bid-ask spreads on cloudy days, suggesting that investors (or market makers) were more risk averse on these days.
- Markets seem to experience significant decline after soccer losses, such as losses in the World Cup elimination stage leading to next-day abnormal stock returns of 0.49%. These loss effects were stronger in small stocks (more likely to be traded by individual investors) and in more important games. They also documented loss effects after international cricket, rugby and basketball games. They controlled for effects of related business revenues resulting from contest outcomes and additionally, did not find that such sports wins had any significant effects on stock returns.
- Scientific evidence is clear that lunar cycles are related to tides, animal behavior and other natural phenomena. In related research drawing on inconsistent research results indicating that homicide rates, hospital admissions, and crisis incidents all peak in the days around full moons, stock returns around new moons nearly double those around full moons.

Simplifying the Decision Process

[C]onsider the simple task of getting dressed in the morning: For a typical male wardrobe of 5 jackets, 10 pants, 20 ties, 10 shirts, 10 pairs of socks, 4 pairs of shoes and 5 belts, there are two million different combinations to evaluate, and if we allow one second to evaluate each outfit, it would take about 23 days to select the "best" outfit ... Yet we all seem to get dressed in just a few minutes — how? [McLeod and Lo]

- Fisher Black in his paper on stock market noise wrote:
  Because there is so much noise in the world, people adopt rules of thumb. They share their rules of thumb with each other, and very few people have enough experience with interpreting noisy evidence to see that the rules are too simple.
- Nevertheless, rules of thumb are important. Without them, many people would be simply unable to invest (or, even get dressed in the morning).

Rational Investors and Diversification

- Perhaps the single most important lesson from modern finance is the importance of diversification and its role in the management of risk.
- Investors do not diversify efficiently.
- A small number of investors have been able to outperform the market by under diversifying. For example, Coval *et al.* [2005] document strong persistence in the performance of trades made by skillful individual investors who seem able to exploit market inefficiencies and information advantages to earn abnormal profits.
- Ivković and Weisbenner [2005] corroborate this result, finding that households exhibit a strong preference for local investments. Ivković and Weisbenner demonstrate that individuals' investments in local stocks outperform their investments in non-local stocks.

D. Neurofinance: Getting into the Investor's Head

- *Neurofinance*, in its infancy stages, is concerned with understanding the neurological processes in the investor's brain as he makes financial decisions.
- Shiv *et al.* [2005] studied the relative abilities of brain-damaged study participants to make gambling decisions.

  - This study gathered 19 subjects that had incurred damage (stable focal lesions) to parts of their brains impairing their abilities to process emotions.
  - The subjects were asked to participate in a series of gambles along with two control groups, one that had experienced no brain damage and a second group that had experienced some other type of brain damage.
  - Each study participant was asked to participate in a sequential series of 20 gambles, betting $1 against a 50/50 chance at either 0 or $2.50. The expected value of each gamble was $1.25, $0.25 higher than its cost.
  - The subjects experiencing damage to their emotional circuitry bet more "normal" counterparts and earned more money.

- The performance differences were more pronounced after non-impaired subjects experienced losses, making them even more reluctant to take advantage of expected wealth-increasing gambles.
- The performance of the emotionally damaged group compared favorably to the control group of participants who had experienced no brain damage and to the second control group who had experienced unrelated types of brain damage.

- In a contrasting study, subjects with similar brain damage (in the ventromedial prefrontal cortex) impairing their abilities to experience emotion seem unable to learn from mistakes in everyday life decisions.

  - Similarly, when faced with repeated losses in "rigged" gambling scenarios, subjects with impaired ability to experience emotions seemed unable to learn from negative experiences.
  - Perhaps, in sum, this and the previous studies suggest that emotions are useful in reacting to negative experiences but can lead to irrational overreactions.

- Lo and Repin [2002] used fMRI to find that more seasoned traders experienced significantly less emotional reaction to dramatic market changes than did their less experienced counterparts.

E. The Consensus Opinion: Stupid Investors, Smart Markets?

- Is it possible for a market consisted of irrational investors to actually, in sum, behave rationally?
- Consider a hypothetical market where professional analysts and competing investors are attempting to secure and employ all information that would enable them to evaluate stocks more accurately. However, none of the analysts have perfect information. Further, assume that each analyst may have some information (or method for analyzing this information) not available to other analysts. However, each analyst may be lacking some information or technique known to his competitors. Thus, information sets available to different analysts are not perfectly correlated. Given a reasonably

large number of analysts, one might expect their errors to offset or cancel to some extent and that their "average" or consensus projections to outperform any given analyst's forecasts.

- Surowiecki [2004] described the popular TV show *Who Wants to be a Millionaire?* to demonstrate the "wisdom of crowds" relative to individual decision makers. In this show, a contestant was asked multiple-choice questions, which, if answered correctly, could result in winnings of as much as $1 million. The contestant had the option ("lifeline") of seeking each of the three types of assistance should he require it. The contestant could request to have two of three incorrect answers eliminated from the answer set, call a friend or relative to ask for help or poll the studio audience who would vote on the correct answer. Eliminating incorrect answers should produce correct answers at least 50% of the time. Phone calls to friends or relatives produced the correct answer almost 65% of the time. However, the studio polls produced the correct answers 91% of the time, suggesting that the crowd wisdom did seem superior to individual opinions, even the potentially expert opinions offered by the phone calls.

- Numerous experiments have demonstrated that averages of class-room estimates of temperatures are more accurate than individual student estimates. Similarly, average estimates provided by surveys produce better estimates of numbers of jelly beans in jars than individual estimates.

The Football Pool

- Sports forecasting and betting provide excellent opportunities for testing market efficiency in that true outcomes are revealed after games are played.

- The *Chicago Daily News* recorded the college football predictions of its sports staff for the last weekend of November during the 1966–1968 seasons.

Analyst Eestimates

- A number of studies have tested analysts' abilities to forecast earnings per share (EPS). Studies have indicated that consensus forecasts for EPS are superior to those of a randomly selected analyst.

- By combining a large number of forecasts, individual analyst idiosyncratic errors will tend to offset one another.
- Several firms make consensus forecasts available to the public, including Lynch, Jones & Ryan's Institutional Brokers Estimate System (IBES), First Call (a subsidiary of Thomson Corporation) and Zacks Investment Research, Inc.

Herds and Swarms

- Markets function without formal leadership or hierarchies.
- Some observers have compared stock markets to swarms of bees and ant colonies.

  - Miller (p. 130) wrote that "Ants aren't clever little engineers, architects, or warriors after all — at least not as individuals."
  - Ants collectively decide how, when and where to forage for food, as, "simple creatures following simple rules, each one acting on local information. No ant tells any other ant what to do. No leadership required."
  - Each ant has a tiny sliver of information that is communicated in a very rudimentary fashion to other ants, but no ant comes close to understanding the "big picture" and no ant can direct the activities of the colony as a whole. Nevertheless, a huge ant colony with hundreds of thousands of ants can thrive, feed itself, reproduce, take care of its young, fight and even enslave other species.

- The stock market may function similarly. Individual traders, each with a subset of information communicates bids and offers. Traders do not reveal their rationale for their quotations, only their quotes. The market collectively sets prices and allocates productive resources throughout the economy. All of this is accomplished without formal leadership or without anyone really understanding exactly why stock prices behave as they do.
- Ivkovic and Weisbenner [2007] find evidence of herding in an examination of 35,000 brokerage accounts detailing investor zip codes.

They found that investors were substantially more likely to invest in securities if their neighbors had already done so. However, markets (and ant colonies as well) may be capable of committing enormous collective blunders, which might be termed bubbles and crashes.

- An *information cascade* is a sequential decision process where each decision maker bases his decision on those made by previous decision makers and then follows his predecessors in the decision-making queue rather than use their own information.

- This information cascading may form the basis for *herd behavior*, where decision makers pursue the same action without collaborative planning. In an information cascade, decision makers earlier in the queue have information relevant to subsequent decision makers, so this herding might be rational.

- The sequential nature of this decision making and its information flow is what characterizes information cascading. But, herd behavior need not be the result of sequential decision making. Members of a herd merely need to exhibit the same behavior without collaborative planning. In fact, herding behavior may seem consistent with collective irrationality. Herding behavior has been blamed for stock market bubbles and crashes.

RANDOM WALKS, RISK AND ARBITRAGE

A. Market Efficiency and Random Walks

- Market efficiency exists when market prices reflect all available information.
- Price changes in an efficient market occur when information changes. Since information dissemination (news) occurs randomly, security price changes might be expected to occur randomly.
- Thus, an efficient market leads to random security price changes.

Random Walk

Random Walks and Martingales

- A *stochastic process* is a sequence of random variables x_t defined on a common probability space (Ω, Φ, P) and indexed by time t.
- The values of $x_t(\omega)$ define the sample path of the process leading to state $\omega \in \Omega$. The terms $x(\omega, t)$, $x_t(\omega)$ and $x(t)$ are synonymous.
- A *discrete time process* is defined for a finite set of time periods; a *continuous time process* is defined over an infinite number of periods.
- The *state space* is the set of values in process $\{x_t\}$:

$$S = \{x \in X_t(\omega) \text{ for } \omega \in \Omega \text{ and some } t\}$$

- A *Markov Process* or *random walk* is a stochastic process whose increments or changes are independent over time, that is, the Markov Process is without memory.
- Let z_i be a random variable associated with time i and let S_t be a state variable (e.g. stock price) at time t, such that $S_t = S_0 + z_1 + z_2 + \cdots + z_t$. Assume that random variables z_i are independent. The discrete time random walk is:

$$E[S_t|S_0, z_1, z_2, \ldots, z_{t-1}] = S_{t-1} + E[z_t]$$

- One type of Markov process, the discrete *martingale process* with $E[z_i] = 0$, is defined with respect to probability measure **P** and history or *filtration* $\Im_{t-1} = \{S_0, z_1, z_2, \ldots, z_{t-1}\}$ as follows:

$$E_P[S_t|S_0, z_1, z_2, \ldots, z_{t-1}] = E_P[S_t|\Im_{t-1}] = S_{t-1}$$

which implies:

$$E_P[S_t|S_0, z_1, z_2, \ldots, z_i] = E_P[S_t|\Im_i] = S_i \quad i < t$$

- Note that $E[z_i] = E[z_t] = 0$. Thus, a martingale is a process whose future variations cannot be predicted with respect to direction based on the process history $\Im_i$. A martingale is said to have no memory and will not exhibit consistent trends.

Brownian Motion Processes

- A *Brownian motion process* is where z is a stochastic process whose changes over infinitesimal periods of time are dz_t. A process z is a standard Brownian motion process if:
  - changes in z over time are independent; $\mathrm{COV}(dz_t, dz_{t-i}) = 0$
  - changes in z are normally distributed with $E[dz] = 0$ and $E[(dz)^2] = 1$; $dz \sim N(0,1)$
  - z is a continuous function of t
  - the process begins at zero, $z_0 = 0$

  Brownian motion:
- is continuous everywhere and differentiable nowhere under Newtonian calculus
- is not smooth and does not become smooth as time intervals decrease

- is a *fractal*
- once a Brownian motion hits a given value, it will return to that value infinitely often over any finite time period, no matter how short
- over a small finite interval, we can express the change in z (i.e. Δz) as follows:

Brownian Motion: A Fractal

Bottom line

- In an efficient market the best estimate of the price tomorrow is the price today
- Prices should follow a random process
- If prices exhibit predictable patterns, we would be able to make money
- In making money, we would "remove" the predictable part of the price movement

Barriers to efficiency

- Efficiency implies that prices reflect all available public information
- This information would include things like fundamentals — earnings, growth rates, etc.
- Some barriers to this could be:

  — Lack of information/announcements
  — Lack of analysts (small stocks)
  — Inability to short sell
  — Not enough money to short sell!

- Famous saying: The market can stay liquid longer than you can stay solvent!

Reasonably well behaved PE ratio average PE ratio > 90x!!! How high does growth need to be? Eventually we see a correction rationality

- If markets are irrational, fundamental investors can push prices back toward their true level

- Even if you are right, it can take a long time for such a correction to eventuate
- To influence the market, you need to be trading with large amounts of money

B. Risk

- One perspective on the risk of an investment is that it is simply the uncertainty associated with investment returns or cash flows.
- However, uncertainty can be a complex quality.
- Analysts often attempt to quantify risk with absolute measures such as variance or relative risk measures such as beta.
- Consider the following discrete expression for *ex-ante* variance that considers all potential return outcomes R_i and associated probabilities P_i:
- While this expression for variance is, by definition correct, its computation requires that we identify all potential returns for the security (which might range from minus infinity to positive infinity) along with their associated probabilities.

Historical Volatility Indicators

- Because it is frequently difficult to estimate the inputs necessary to estimate security *ex-ante* variance, analysts often use the volatility of *ex-post* or historical returns as a surrogate for *ex-ante* risk.
- Use of the traditional sample estimator to forecast variance requires the assumption that stock return variances are constant over time, or more specifically, that historical return variance is an appropriate indicator of future return variance.
- While this can often be a reasonable assumption, firm risk conditions can change and it is well documented that price volatility does fluctuate over time (see, for example, Officer [1971]).
- Using this equation to estimate security variance requires that the analyst choose a sample series of prices (and dividends, if relevant) at n regular intervals from which to compute returns. Two problems arise in this process:

  — Which prices should be selected and at what intervals?
  — How many prices should be selected?

Realized Volatility — EDE

- March 2013–March 2015

Realized Volatility — EDE

- March 2013–September 2016

Extreme Value Estimators

- The Parkinson Extreme Value Estimator is based on the assumption that underlying stock returns are log-normally distributed without drift.
- Given this distribution assumption, the underlying stock's realized high and low prices over a given period provide information regarding the stock's variance:

Implied Volatilities

- A problem shared by both the traditional sample estimating procedures and the extreme value estimators is that they require the assumption of stable variance estimates over time; more specifically, that future variances equal or can be estimated from historical variances.
- Another procedure is based on market prices of options that might be used to imply variance estimates. For example, the Black–Scholes Option Pricing Model provides an excellent means to estimate underlying stock variances if call prices are known.
- Essentially, this procedure determines market estimates for underlying stock variance based on known market prices for options on the underlying securities.

Basic Risk Measures

C. Arbitrage

- Arbitrage is the simultaneous purchase and sale of assets or portfolios yielding identical cash flows.

- Assets generating identical cash flows (certain or risky cash flows) should be worth the same amount. This is the *Law of One Price.*
- If assets generating identical cash flows sell at different prices, opportunities exist to create a profit by buying the cheaper asset and selling the more expensive asset.
- Rational investors in such a scenario will seek to purchase the underpriced asset, financing its purchase by simultaneously selling the overpriced asset. The *arbitrageur* will execute such arbitrage transactions, continuing to earn arbitrage profits in increasing quantities until the arbitrage opportunity is eliminated.
- *Classic arbitrage* is the simultaneous purchase and sale of the same asset at a profit.
- For example, if gold is selling in London markets for $1,600 per ounce and in New York markets for $1,620 per ounce, a classic arbitrage opportunity exists. An investor could purchase gold in London for $1,600 per ounce and simultaneously sell it in New York for $1,620. This results in a $20 profit per "round trip" transaction.
- The transactions involve no risk since both the selling and purchase prices are known and are executed simultaneously. Furthermore, no initial net investment is required because the transactions offset each other; the proceeds of the sale are used to finance the purchase.
- Perhaps an even simpler form of arbitrage opportunity exists in a *crossed market*, where a bid exceeds an offer price. This can occur when a slow trader's quote is not withdrawn quickly enough, enabling a prospective buyer to purchase a security at the lower offer price and immediately sell it at the higher bid price.
- More generally, arbitrage refers to the near simultaneous purchase and sale of portfolios generating similar cash flow structures.
- For example, the cash flow structure of a long position in a forward contract can be replicated by a portfolio consisting of a long position in a call and short position in a put. Although the contracts in the options portfolio are different from the forward contract, the anticipated cash flows are identical.
- The principle of arbitrage is the foundation underlying relative securities valuation.

- That is, we are able to price securities relative to one another or relative to replicating portfolios when arbitrageurs are able to exploit violations of the Law of One Price.

Pairs Trading and Stat-Arb

- *Pairs trading* involves the simultaneous purchase and sale of similar securities. Pairs traders take offsetting positions of two different, but strongly correlated stocks (perhaps options or index contracts) such that gains in one position are expected to be more than offset losses in the other position.
- One simple strategy illustration might involve taking a long position in General Motors (GM) stock based on recent price decreases along with a short position in Ford based on recent price increases. Pairs trading is essentially a strategy anticipating that the deviation of a recent pricing relation is only temporary.
- Holding periods for most pairs trading strategies tend to be quite short. Pairs traders typically focus either on the ratio between prices of two securities or the difference between their prices.
- One cannot expect to consistently earn high returns based on such strategies, so that many pairs traders execute many such trades over many different pairs with the expectation that their strategies will be correct more often than they are wrong.
- Furthermore, many pairs traders will seek to hold "portfolios of pairs" whose expected returns will tend to be uncorrelated with the market. Such "beta neutral" portfolios might be expected to be insulated from large losses related to stock market swings.
- In a manner similar to pairs trading, *stat-arb* (statistical arbitrage) strategies seek to exploit mispricing opportunities while minimizing risk.
- Stat-arb strategies focus on statistical or historical relationships among securities and seek to exploit price divergences as portfolios of securities diverge from "normal" pricing relationships.
- There is no single stat-arb strategy; there are many types, all of which involve large sets of securities whose statistical price relationships relative to each other diverge from what the investor expects.

D. Limits to Arbitrage

- Risks associated with arbitrage include:

  — *implementation risk* because transactions might not be executed, might only be partly executed or be executed at prices that differ from what was anticipated.

  — *model risk* arising from a simple failure to appreciate the differences between model assumptions and reality.

  — *basis risk* where prices move contrary to expectations, worsening cash flows, leading to margin calls, etc. Mitigated by holding assets to maturity.

  — *counterparty risk*, which is the potential that a trade counterparty fails to fulfill their side of a transaction.

Negative Stub Values

- In March 2000 equity carve-out, 3Com spun off its Palm division, a maker of handheld computers.

  — 3Com retained 95% of the shares of Palm and each 3Com shareholder received 1.5 shares of Palm for each share of 3Com.

  — The remaining 5% of Palm shares were issued at $38 per share, increasing to $165 by its first day of trading before closing at $95.06.

  — Ownership of one 3Com share implied ownership of 1.5 shares of Palm stock.

  — The stocks should have moved in tandem, but on the date of the IPO, 3Com actually decreased by 21% to $81.81.

  — This $81.81 is substantially less than the $142.59 price implied by the 1.5 shares of Palm stock ($1.5 \cdot \$95.06 = \$142.59$), implying that the remainder of 3Com, on a per share basis, was worth negative $60.78.

  — This negative stub value (the whole is worth less than the sum of the parts) seems particularly unlikely, since 3Com had about $10 per share in cash and marketable securities alone.

  — However, prospective arbitrageurs found themselves unable to short sell shares because the two stocks were under different national regulatory authorities. Thus, arbitrage and price correction could not be implemented because the short selling mechanism was not available for the Palm IPO.

- Such negative stub values are not uncommon.
  - In 1923, Benjamin Graham chronicled his purchase of shares of stock in Du Pont, a well-established firm that had negative stub value given its investment in the new company General Motors.
  - Lamont and Thaler [2001] identified five other 1990s technology equity carve-outs with negative stub values: UBID, Retek, PFSWeb, Xpedior and Stratos Lightwave. Arbitrage in each of these cases was impeded by the inability to short sell.
  - Mitchell *et al.* [2002] found 82 similar instances in the US markets between 1985 and 2000. But in most cases, arbitrage was impeded by inability to short sell, high transactions costs and difficulty in getting reliable price quotes or other information. But, Mitchell *et al.* found that approximately 30% of negative stub values were never eliminated through arbitrage. Some of the spin-offs failed, and others may have faced this risk. But, even this probably cannot explain particularly large negative stub values.

Constraints to Arbitrage

- TAS owns 493 million shares in EDE
- TAS also owns 101 million EDE options exercisable at 3c before 2018
- There are 393 million TAS shares on issue
- This means there are 1.297 EDE shares/TAS
- There are also 0.265 EDEO/TAS

Prices? As of September 8, 2016

- TAS: 17.5c
- EDE: 25c
- EDEO: 22c
- Value of TAS shareholding in EDE?

- 38.1c
- So, should not we buy!?!?

Share Prices Relative Shareprices Constraints

- Ideally, I would want to sell EDE and buy TAS
- Then my investments would be perfectly correlated
- However, I cannot short EDE (let me know if you figure out how!?!?)
- So, best I can do is go long in TAS
- This is not arbitrage, however
- Prices may never converge

Informed Trading

- Information is impounded in prices when people trade
- This information could be public or private
- Both will incorporate information by moving the price

Price Spiked BEFORE Mining Discovery

Price Query

- On May 13, ASX issued a price query to see if any information could explain price spike
- PIO said they had nothing to disclose
- Six days later they announced they had found lithium (for your mobile batteries)

Firms almost always say they know nothing
Days till next announcement
Most announcements to do with... Drilling!

ARBITRAGE IN REAL TRADING MARKETS AND HEDGING

Arbitrage

- Arbitrage is the simultaneous purchase and sale of assets or portfolios yielding identical cash flows.
- Assets generating identical cash flows (certain or risky cash flows) should be worth the same amount. This is the *Law of One Price*.
- If assets generating identical cash flows sell at different prices, opportunities exist to create a profit by buying the cheaper asset and selling the more expensive asset.
- Rational investors in such a scenario will seek to purchase the underpriced asset, financing its purchase by simultaneously selling the overpriced asset. The *arbitrageur* will execute such arbitrage transactions, continuing to earn arbitrage profits in increasing quantities until the arbitrage opportunity is eliminated.
- *Classic arbitrage* is the simultaneous purchase and sale of the same asset at a profit.
- For example, if gold is selling in London markets for $1,600 per ounce and in New York markets for $1,620 per ounce, a classic arbitrage opportunity exists. An investor could purchase gold in London for $1,600 per ounce and simultaneously sell it in New York for $1,620. This results in a $20 profit per "round trip" transaction.
- The transactions involve no risk since both the selling and purchase prices are known and are executed simultaneously. Furthermore, no initial net investment is required because the transactions

offset each other; the proceeds of the sale are used to finance the purchase.

- Perhaps an even simpler form of arbitrage opportunity exists in a *crossed market*, where a bid exceeds an offer price. This can occur when a slow trader's quote is not withdrawn quickly enough, enabling a prospective buyer to purchase a security at the lower offer price and immediately sell it at the higher bid price.

- More generally, arbitrage refers to the near simultaneous purchase and sale of portfolios generating similar cash flow structures.

- For example, the cash flow structure of a long position in a forward contract can be replicated by a portfolio consisting of a long position in a call and short position in a put. Although the contracts in the options portfolio are different from the forward contract, the anticipated cash flows are identical.

- Arbitrage is the foundation underlying relative securities valuation.

- That is, we are able to price securities relative to one another or relative to replicating portfolios when arbitrageurs are able to exploit violations of the Law of One Price.

Does Pure Arbitrage Exist?

- Yes, for ultra-short intervals!

- Research Paper: This chapter shows that when we analyze sufficiently detailed data short-lived violations (Covered Interest Rate Parity), the law of one price occurs which are traded on by currency dealers until they disappear. The results show the proportion of profitable deviations, how large in pips and duration.

Pairs Trading and Stat-Arb

- *Pairs trading* involves the simultaneous purchase and sale of similar securities. Pairs traders take offsetting positions two different, but strongly correlated stocks (perhaps options or index contracts) such that gains in one position are expected to more than offset losses in the other position.

- One simple strategy illustration might involve taking a long position in GM stock based on recent price decreases along with a short position in Ford based on recent price increases. Pairs trading is essentially a strategy anticipating that the deviation of a recent pricing relation is only temporary.

- Holding periods for most pairs trading strategies tend to be quite short. Pairs traders typically focus either on the ratio between prices of two securities or the difference between their prices.
- One cannot expect to consistently earn high returns based on such strategies, so that many pairs traders execute many such trades over many different pairs with the expectation that their strategies will be correct more often than they are wrong.
- Furthermore, many pairs traders will seek to hold "portfolios of pairs" whose expected returns will tend to be uncorrelated with the market. Such "beta neutral"
- portfolios might be expected to be insulated from large losses related to stock market swings.
- In a manner similar to pairs trading, *stat-arb* (statistical arbitrage) strategies seek to exploit mis-pricing opportunities while minimizing risk.
- Stat-arb strategies focus on statistical or historical relationships among securities and seek to exploit price divergences as portfolios of securities diverge from "normal" pricing relationships.
- There is no single stat-arb strategy; there are many types, all of which involve large sets of securities whose statistical price relationships relative to each other diverge from what the investor expects.
- **Example of pairs trading**
- http://www.investopedia.com/university/guide-pairs-trading/pairs-trade-example.asp

Recap of Teall Chapter 6

Limits to Arbitrage

- Risks associated with arbitrage include:
  - *implementation risk* because transactions might not be executed, might only be partly executed or be executed at prices that differ what was anticipated.

— *model risk* arising from a simple failure to appreciate the differences between model assumptions and reality.

— *basis risk* where prices move contrary to expectations, worsening cash flows, leading to margin calls, etc. Mitigated by holding assets to maturity.

— *counterparty risk*, which is the potential that a trade counterparty fails to fulfill their side of a transaction.

Derivative Securities Markets and Hedging

A derivative security is simply a financial instrument whose value is derived from that of another security, financial index or rate.

- Options
- Futures Contracts
- Swaps
- Hybrids
- **Derivatives is the fastest growing area in trading, where human analytical skills are highly desirable.**
- **Market making** is a necessary function for option markets to function
- Some of these functions can be automated by **algorithms**, but designing and operating this program requires highly specialized individuals

Put-Call Parity

$$p_T = \text{MAX}[0, X - S_T]$$
$$c_T - p_T = \text{MAX}[0, S_T - X] - \text{MAX}[0, X - S_T] = S_T - X$$
$$p_T = c_T + X - S_T$$

Options and Hedging in a Binomial Environment

- *The Binomial Option Pricing Model* is based on the assumption that the underlying stock follows a binomial return generating process
- This means that for any period during the life of the option, the stock's value will be only one of the two potential constant values

Valuing the One-Period Option

Extending the Binomial Model to Two Periods

- First, we substitute for the hedge ratio:
- Some algebra then substitutes hedging probabilities:

Two Time Periods

Extending the Binomial Model to n Time Periods

Illustration: Three Time Periods

Obtaining multiplicative upward and downward movement values

- One difficulty in applying the binomial model is obtaining estimates for u and d that are required for p; all other inputs are normally quite easily obtained.

Convergence of the Binomial Model to the Black–Scholes Model

- Table 8.1 (pp. 207–209 of *Binomial Model: An Illustration*)

The Greeks and Hedging in a Black–Scholes Environment

- **Black–Scholes Illustration**

$$T = 0.5 \quad r_f = 0.10$$
$$X = 80 \quad \sigma^2 = 0.16$$
$$\sigma = 0.4 \quad S_0 = 75$$

- **Greeks Calculation, pp. 213–214**

Delta Neutral Hedging

- Weekly rebalancing of a delta neutral hedge obtains a remarkably good result!
- Solution example in Excel Table on BB
- **Hedging for Delta and Gamma Neutrality, pp. 214–215**

- Same example as above, but add a call with $X = 75$
- We skip 8.5 Exchange Options
- What we have learned applies to these also, but we have two interest rates, r_d domestic and r_f foreign. Not examinable but pretty interesting and useful to learn!

Example Real Option Prices

- A typical trading screen for an options trader
- Definition of call, put, buying, writing, a contract, option series (a specific set of calls or puts on the same underlying security, in the same class and with the same strike price and expiration date = casually "one option")
- What is the underlying contract size (specified by the exchange)?
- How are the strike prices and expiry dates determined? When are they adjusted?
- Which expiry has the best liquidity and when do traders roll-over to the next period?

Example Real Option Prices

- The trader has chosen not to display the B&S (theoretical) price rather implied volatilities.
- Find the mispriced option series!

Recap Chapter 6: Implied Volatilities

- A problem shared by both the traditional sample estimating procedures and the extreme value estimators is that they require the assumption of stable variance estimates over time; more specifically, that future variances equal or can be estimated from historical variances.
- Another procedure is based on market prices of options that might be used to imply variance estimates. For example, the Black–Scholes Option Pricing Model provide an excellent means to estimate underlying stock variances if call prices are known.

- Essentially, this procedure determines market estimates for underlying stock variance based on known market prices for options on the underlying securities.
- **Other Derivatives**
- Futures
- Exchange-traded options [ETO] versus OTC
- Swaps
- Hybrid
- ETFs not classified as a derivative, but in practice has some features of a derivative as they are constructed to track an index, a security or commodity. They trade like a derivative with tracking error.

MARKET EFFICIENCY

Introduction to Market Efficiency

- An Efficient Capital Market is a market where security prices reflect all available information.

- In an efficient market, the expected price of a tradable asset, given the information φ available to the market and the information φ_k available to any investor k, equals the expected price based on the information available to the market for all investors k:

- The price of the asset reflects the consensus evaluation of the market based on the information available to the market, regardless of private information held by investor k.

- Individual k's information set φ_k does not improve his estimate of expected price in an efficient market; the market price already reflects all relevant information φ including investor k's special information φ_k.

- In a perfectly efficient market where security prices fully reflect all available information, all security transactions will have zero net present value.

Weak Form Efficiency

- *Weak form efficiency tests* are concerned with whether an investor might consistently earn higher than normal returns based on knowledge of historical price sequences.

- One can never prove weak form efficiency because there are an infinite number of ways to forecast future returns from past returns.

- Cowles [1933] and Working [1934] studied the random movement of stock prices. Their results indicated that stock prices seemed to fluctuate randomly, without being influenced by their histories.
- Another of the earlier weak form efficiency tests found a very slight, but statistically significant relationship between historical and current prices: 0.057% of a given day's variation in the log of the price relative is explained by the prior day's change in the log of the price relative.
- The r-squared value from one such regression was 0.00057, where represents price of stock i on a given day t, the price on the day immediately prior, b_0 and b_1 regression coefficients and the error terms in the regression.

Residuals Tests

- Fama and MacBeth, after adjusting for risk, found no correlation in daily capital asset pricing model (CAPM) residuals.
- Error terms are regressed against their prior day values. A negative value for b_i suggests mean reversion. Positive values for b_i suggest momentum. Fama and MacBeth found very little evidence for either mean reversion or momentum in stock prices.

Runs Tests

- It is important to note that correlation coefficients can be unduly influenced by extreme observations. One way to deal with such assumption violations is to construct a simple runs test.
- Consider the following daily price sequence: 50, 51, 52, 53, 52, 50, 45, 49, 54 and 53. The price changes might be represented by the following: (+ + + +—++-), indicating four price runs. That is, there were four series of positive or negative price change runs. The expected number of runs in a runs test if price changes are random is (MAX + MIN)/2, where MAX is the largest number of possible runs (equals the number of prices in the series) and MIN is the minimum number (1).

- The number of runs consistent with random sequences in our example is $10 = (9+1)/2$. More runs suggest mean reversion and a smaller number suggests momentum.
- The actual levels of returns are unimportant; only the signs of returns are important, so that extreme observations will not unduly bias tests. In one test of daily price changes, Fama [1965] expected 760 runs based on the assumption that price changes were randomly generated, but only found 735 runs. High transactions costs seem to be related to runs — investors are unable to exploit a series because of brokerage commissions.
- Two to three times as many reversals of price trends as continuations based on transaction-to-transaction price data. This might be because of unexecuted limit orders — for them to be executed the price has to reverse itself. For example, suppose that a market purchase order has just been executed at an uptick. All of the limit sell orders at this most recent execution price have to be executed for the price to increase again. This means that a purchase is more likely to be followed by a downtick $(-)$ or no change at all (0) than an uptick $(+)$.

Filter Rules and Market Over-reaction

- A filter rule states that a transaction for a security should occur when its price has changed by a given percentage over a specified period of time.
- Some early studies found that when filter rules did seem to work (however slightly), they were not able to cover transactions costs. Profitability of these rules seem to be related to daily correlations.
- Such correlation and filter rules seemed to work slightly better in Norway, where stronger correlations tended to exist. However, these markets were less liquid and transactions costs were significantly higher in Norwegian markets than in American markets.
- DeBondt and Thaler [1985] argued that buying stocks that performed poorly in a prior 3–5 year period and selling those that performed well would have generated abnormally high returns in subsequent 3–5 year periods.

- On the other hand, Jegadeesh and Titman [1993] found results that conflicted with DeBondt and Thaler based on shorter holding periods (3–12 months). Their study suggested that the market is slow to react to firm-specific information.
- The findings of both DeBondt and Thaler and Jegadeesh and Titman that seem to contradict weak form market efficiency are not universally accepted. For example, Richardson and Stock [1988] argued that these momentum results of DeBondt and Thaler were due largely to their statistical methodology, as did Jegadeesh [1991] who argued that these mean reversion effects seemed to hold only in January.

Moving Averages

- *Moving average* techniques consolidate shorter series of observations into longer series and are used for smoothing data variability.
- A simple q-period moving average is computed as follows:
- Trading strategies might be based on these moving averages. For example, if current prices rise above a falling moving average, they might be expected to drop back toward the moving average; selling is suggested.
- Moving averages can be computed for any number of price data points. For example, consider the following sequence of daily closing prices for a given stock over a period of time:

12	14	17	
13	14	19	22
17	11	18	16
22			
$t = 1$	$t = 2$	$t = 3$	
$t = 4$	$t = 5$	$t = 6$	
$t = 7$	$t = 8$	$t = 9$	
$t = 10$	$t = 11$	$t = 12$	

- The following represents the sequence of simple 3-day moving averages for the above price sequences:

NA	NA	14.3	
14.7	14.7	15.3	
18.3	19.3	16.7	
15.3	15.0	18.7	
$t = 1$	$t = 2$	$t = 3$	$t = 4$
$t = 5$	$t = 6$	$t = 7$	
$t = 8$	$t = 9$	$t = 10$	
$t = 11$	$t = 12$		

- Brock *et al.* [1992] demonstrated evidence suggesting that certain moving average rules and regulations based on resistance levels produced higher than normal returns when applied to daily data for the Dow Jones Industrial Average from 1897 to 1986. However, Sullivan *et al.* [1997] tested their findings on updated data and found "that the best technical trading rule does not provide superior performance when used to trade in the subsequent 10-year post-sample period."

Moving Average Example

The January Effect

- Numerous studies have confirmed a "January Effect," where returns for the month of January tend to exceed returns for other months.
- This January effect has a greater effect on the shares of smaller companies (which are frequently held by individual investors) than on shares of larger firms (frequently held by institutional investors).
- Some studies suggest that much of the January effect can be explained by December transactions being seller initiated and execute at bids, while January transactions are buyer initiated and

execute at offers. However, the January effect is large enough that it would exist even if all transactions executed at bids.

- The January Effect and Tax-driven Selling

  — Year-end tax selling — investors selling their "losers" at the end of the year to capture tax write-offs may force down prices at the end of the year. They recover early in the following year, most significantly during the first five trading days in January (and the last trading day in December).
  — Abnormally high trading volume exists in December.
  — "Losers" outperform "winners" in January of the subsequent year.
  — January effects exist for low grade corporate bonds and in shares of companies that issue these bonds. This effect does not seem to hold for high grade corporate bonds or for the shares of the companies that issue these bonds.

- Contrasting tax explanations are studies demonstrating that this effect exists in markets whose tax years differ from the calendar year.
- The January effect appears in Australia and other countries where the fiscal and calendar years differ. The January effect in Canada existed before the introduction of a capital gains tax.
- The US markets might be sufficiently influential in world markets that year-end tax selling in the US might simply drive prices in other markets.
- On the other hand, there was a January effect in the US markets during 1877–1916, before the US income taxes. Again, a January effect with no tax-driven selling.
- Furthermore, municipal bond issues, which are free from federal taxation, experience a significant January effect.

The January Effect and Window-Dressing

- Funds may "window dress" at year-end by buying winners (stocks that performed well earlier in the year) and by selling losers. These transactions occur at the end of the year so that their clientele can see from year-end financial statements that their funds held high-performing stocks and did not hold losers.

- However, most institutions report their holdings to clients more than once per year. But, this effect does not appear in any other month. Furthermore, winners still realize higher January returns than in any other month; just not as high as losers.
- If the "window-dressing" hypothesis explains the January effect better than the tax-selling hypothesis, one should expect that shares held by institutions should outperform shares held by individuals during the month of January.
- The January effect is more pronounced for smaller firms than for larger firms (smaller firms are more likely to be held by individual investors).
- The January effect is more pronounced for companies with many individual shareholders than companies with more institutional investors.

The Small Firm and P/E Effects

- The stock of smaller firms may outperform larger firms.
- This effect may hold after adjusting for risk as measured by beta.
- However, other measures of risk may be more appropriate for smaller firms that may not have well-established trading records.
- Furthermore, transactions costs for many smaller firms may exceed those for larger firms, particularly when they are thinly traded.
- The small firm effect seems most pronounced in January.
- Although Fama and French [1992] find a significant size effect in their study of the CAPM over a 50-year period, they do not find a size effect during the period between 1981 and 1990. This *might* suggest that the size effect either no longer exists or was merely a statistical artifact prior to 1981.
- Basu [1977] and Fama and French [1992] find that firms with low price to earnings ratios outperform firms with higher P/E ratios.
- Fama and French find that the P/E ratio, combined with firm size predict security returns significantly better than the CAPM.

The IPO Anomaly

- The IPO anomaly refers to patterns associated with Initial Public Offerings (IPOs) of equities:

  1. Short-term IPO returns are abnormally high.
  2. IPOs seem to underperform the market in the long run.
  3. IPO underperformance seems to be cyclical.

Australian IPOs Performance

Sports betting markets

- Sports betting markets potentially have much in common with stock markets. There is some evidence of persistent inefficiencies in sports betting markets. For example, Thaler and Ziemba [1988] note that favorites in horse races outperform long shots while Woodland and Woodland [1994] find the opposite is true for baseball betting. Brown and Sauer [1993] find that several observable variables in addition to the spread can be used to improve the outcomes of professional basketball games. Gray and Gray [1997], Golec and Tamarkin [1991] and Gandar *et al.* [1988] find evidence that certain strategies can be used to improve professional football betting.

Summary

- Generally, statistical studies indicate that stock markets are efficient with respect to historical price sequences.
- However, one must realize that an infinite number of possible sequences can be identified with any series of prices. Clearly, many of these series must be associated with higher than normal future returns.
- However, when research finds a sequence that leads to higher than normal returns, one must question whether the abnormal return result is merely a statistical artifact due to data mining. William Schwert [2003] was quoted:

  These [research] findings raise the possibility that anomalies are more apparent than real. The notoriety associated with the findings of unusual evidence tempts authors to further investigate puzzling anomalies and later try to explain them. But even if the anomalies existed in the sample period in which they were first identified, the activities of practitioners who implement strategies to take advantage of anomalous behavior can cause the anomalies to disappear (as research findings cause the market to become more efficient).

- Richard Roll [1992], in a blunt comment, stated:
  I have personally tried to invest money, my client's and my own, in every single anomaly and predictive result that academics have dreamed up. That includes the strategy of DeBondt and Thaler (that is, sell short individual stocks immediately after one-day increases of more than 5%), the reverse of DeBondt and Thaler which is Jegadeesh and Titman (buy individual stocks after they have decreased by 5%), etc. I have attempted to exploit the so-called year-end anomalies and a whole variety of strategies supposedly documented by academic research. And I have yet to make a nickel on any of these supposed market inefficiencies.

- Clearly, technical analysis has its share of critics. Warren Buffet was quoted saying, "I realized technical analysis didn't work when I turned the charts upside down and didn't get a different answer."

- Most apparent incidences of mispricing seem eliminated by transactions costs. The primary exceptions to weak form market efficiency seem to be the IPO effect, probably the January effect, perhaps the small firm effect, and perhaps the P/E effect.

- There is little agreement as to why these effects persist or even if the latter two do exist, they are anomalies.

Semi-Strong Form Efficiency

- *Semi-strong form efficiency* tests are concerned with whether security prices reflect all publicly available information.

- For example, how much time is required for a given type of information to be reflected in security prices? What types of publicly available information might an investor use to generate higher than normal returns?

- The vast majority of studies of semi-strong form market efficiency suggest that the tested publicly available information and announcements cannot be used by the typical investor to secure significantly higher than normal returns.

Early Tests

- Cox [1930] found no evidence that professional stock analysts could outperform the market.
- Cowles [1933] performed several tests of what was later to be known as the efficient market hypothesis (EMH). He examined the forecasting abilities of 45 professional securities analysis agencies, comparing the returns that might have been generated by professionals' recommendations to actual returns on the market over the same period.

  — Average returns generated by professionals were less than those generated by the market over the same periods.
  — The best performing fund did not exhibit unusually high performance at a statistically significant level.
  — Cowles also tested whether analyst picks were more profitable than random picks.
  — Cowles examined the abilities of analysts to predict the direction of the market as opposed to selecting individual stocks.
  — A buy and hold strategy was no less profitable than following advice of professionals as to when to long or short the market.
  — He performed a simulation study using a deck of cards. Based on reports of analyst recommendations, he computed the average number of times analysts change their recommendations over a year. He then randomly selected dates, using cards numbered 1–229 (the number of weeks the study covered) to make simulated random recommendations. Draws were taken from a second set of randomly selected cards numbered 1–9, each with a certain recommendation (long, short, half stock and half cash, etc.) for a given date. Cowles then compared the results distribution of the 33 recommendations based on randomly generated advice to the advice provided by the actual

advisors. He found that the professionals generated the same return distributions as did the random recommendations.

— Cowles also examined 255 editorials by William Peter Hamilton, the fourth editor of the *Wall Street Journal* who had a reputation for successful forecasting. Between 1902 until his death 1929, Hamilton forecast 90 changes in the market; 45 were correct and 45 were incorrect.

- If experts are unable to distinguish between strong and weak stock market performers, and investors are well aware of this lack of ability, why do market forecasters still exist and investors still purchase and follow their advice?
- One possible explanation for reliance on unreliable "expert" forecasters is that investors are less interested in accuracy than in avoiding responsibility for their selections.

  — Investors who rely on advice from experts seek to avoid blame when the forecasts are inaccurate.
  — Avoidance of responsibility in another field is illustrated by Cocozza and Steadman [1978] in their study of New York psychiatrists who were asked to predict whether mental patients were dangerous and required involuntary confinement.

FFJR, Stock Splits and Event Studies

- FFJR examined the effects of stock splits on stock prices.

  — This paper was the first to use the now classic event study methodology.
  — Although stock prices did change significantly before announcements of stock splits (and afterwards as well), Fama *et al.* argued that splits were related to more fundamental factors (such as dividends), and that it was actually these fundamental factors that affected stock prices. The splits themselves were unimportant with respect to subsequent returns.
  — Fama *et al.* identified the month in which a particular stock split occurred, calling that month time zero for that stock. Thus, each stock had associated with it a particular month

zero $(t = 0)$, and months subsequent to the split were assigned positive values.

— They estimated expected returns for each month t for the stocks in their sample with single index model: $r_{i,t} = a + b_i r_{m,t} + e_{i,t}$ where the expected residual $(e_{i,t})$ value was zero.

— They examined residuals $(e_{i,t})$ for each security i for each month t then averaged the residuals (AR_t) for each month across securities.

— Afterwards, they calculated cumulative average residuals (CAR_t) starting 30 months before splits $(t = -30)$.

— FFJR provided the framework for future event studies and semi-strong efficiency tests.

• Consider the following general notes regarding testing the semi-strong form efficiency hypothesis:

— Use daily price and returns data since information is incorporated into prices within days (or much shorter periods).

— Announcements are usually more important than events themselves.

— Base security performance on estimated expected returns.

— When using Standard Single Index Model, we estimate slopes from historical data. Normally, we find them biased forecasters for future values, so we may adjust them toward one.

— One way to deal with slope measurement error is to use moving windows.

— An alternative to CARs is buy and hold abnormal residuals as follows: $BHAR_t = \Pi(1 + e_t) - 1$.

Corporate Merger Announcements, Annual Reports and Other Financial Statements

• Firth considered market efficiency when an announcement is made for purchase of more than 10% of a firm.

— Presumably, an announcement indicates a potential merger.

— Firth calculated CAR starting 30 days prior to announcements; the bulk of CAR is realized between last trade before and first trade after announcements, though it still increases slightly after an announcement.

— Thus, a large block purchaser can still make excess returns.
— An insider obviously can make excess returns; one without inside information cannot (except for the first trader after the announcement).
— Since returns change almost immediately, Firth suggested that there is a semi-strong efficiency with respect to merger announcements.

- Ball and Brown [1968] study the usefulness of the information content of annual reports.

  — With a primary focus on EPS, they find that security prices already reflect 85–90% of information contained in annual reports
  — Security prices show no consistent reactions to annual report releases

Information Contained in Publications and Analyst Reports

- Davies and Canes [1978] considered information analysts sell to clients, then publish in the "Heard on the Street" column in *The Wall Street Journal*. Prices seem to rise significantly after information is sold to clients, then even more when it is published in *The Wall Street Journal*.
- Other studies have been performed on the ability to use information provided by Value Line Investment Surveys to generate profits.
- More general studies on the value of analyst reports are somewhat mixed.

  — The earlier study by Cowles [1933] found no evidence of value in analyst reports.
  — Green [2005] found that short-term profit opportunities persist for 2 h following the pre-market release of new recommendations.

- Womack [1996] found that analysts' mean post-event drift averages 2.4% on buy recommendations and is short lived. However, sell recommendations result in average losses of 9.1% that are longer lived. These price reactions seem more significant for small-capitalization firms than for larger capitalization firms. Also, consider that sell recommendations may be particularly costly to brokerage firms, potentially damaging investment banking relationships and curtailing access to information in the future. Clearly, buy recommendations far outnumber sell recommendations and an incorrect sell recommendation may be particularly damaging to an analyst's reputation.
- See for further details Chordiya *et al.* [2016].

Analyst Reports and Conflicts of Interest

- Michaely and Womack [1999] attempted to discern whether analysts working for firms underwriting the IPOs provided buy recommendations that were superior to those of investment institutions not participating in the underwriting efforts.
- Results suggest that if the analyst worked for an institution that did not participate in the underwriting, they were more likely to recommend a stock that had performed well in the recent past and would continue its strong performance.
- However, if the analyst worked for a firm that participated in bringing the IPO to the market, it was more likely to have recorded poor performance both before and after the analyst's recommendation.
- This evidence suggests that analysts working for investment banks are likely to attempt to prop up the prices of their underwritten securities with their recommendations.
- In response to these apparently biased and unethical analyst recommendations, the Securities and Exchange Commission (SEC) announced in 2003 the Global Research Analyst Settlement with 10 of the industry's largest investment banks. The settlement required the 10 investment banks to pay $875 million in penalties and profit disgorgement, $80 million for investor education

and \$432.5 million to fund independent research. In addition to these payments, the investment banks were required to separate their investment banking and research departments and add certain disclosures to their research reports.

- Nevertheless, Barber *et al.* [2007] find that investment bank buy opinions still underperform those of independent analysts, despite their other recommendations outperforming those of their independent competitors.

DCF Analysis and Price Multiples

- In their study of 51 highly leveraged transactions (management buyouts and leveraged recapitalizations), Kaplan and Ruback [1995] found that DCF analysis provided better estimates of value than did price-based multiples.
- Kaplan and Ruback found that between 95% and 97% of firm value was explained by (as indicated by r-square) DCF and slightly less was explained by price-based multiples.
- The price-based multiples did add useful information to the valuation process.

Political Intelligence Units

- Investors with money at stake have obvious incentives to access and quickly exploit information.
- Many investors and institutions are able to access and exploit important information before it can be gathered and disseminated by the news agencies.
- Consider the case of USG Corporation, whose shares increased by 5.4% over 2 days prior to November 16, 2005 when Senate Republican Majority Leader Bill Frist announced that there would be a full Senate vote on a bill to create a \$140 billion public trust for asbestos liability claims.

  — This fund would pay medical expenses and resolve lawsuits involving thousands of cancer victims who blamed USG, W.R. Grace and Crown for their illnesses.

— Share prices of all these firms increased over the 2 days prior to November 16.
— Returns for these firms over the 2-day period exceeded those of the market.
— In addition, returns experienced by these particular firms far exceeded returns of their peer firms that were not involved in asbestos litigation.
— On the date that the actual announcement was finally made, these three firms showed no substantial reaction.

- The SEC initiated an informal investigation to determine whether and how information might have been leaked to investors prior to its announcement.
- While staff members for Senator Frist claim to have been careful not to leak information prior to the announcement, the bill's authors, Senators Spector and Leahy had held extensive discussions with lobbyists.
- Several law firms, including Sonnenschein Nath & Rosenthal, LLP and DLA Piper have operated "political intelligence" units enabling their clients to obtain public policy information from lobbyists operating in Washington. These firms and political intelligence units include hedge funds as clients.
- Several hedge funds holding substantial stakes in affected companies belonged to the Financial Institutions for Asbestos Reform, an industry advocacy group, giving them additional opportunities to access information provided by lobbyists.
- While it is not clear whether any laws were have been broken, it does appear that hedge funds may have successfully gained an information edge in their trading.

Market Volatility

- If security price changes are purely a function of information arrival, then security price volatility should be the same when markets are closed as when they are open.
- For example, stock return variances should be three times as high over a weekend as over a 24-h period during weekdays.

- However, Fama [1965] and French [1980] found that return variances were only around 20% higher during weekends.
- On the other hand, one might argue that the arrival of new information over weekends is slower.
- Another study by French and Roll [1986] found that agricultural commodity futures prices (orange juice concentrate) were substantially more volatile during trading days than during weekends.
- Agricultural commodity futures prices are primarily a function of weather, news about which occurs over the weekend just as efficiently as during trading days.

Strong Form Efficiency and Insider Trading

- Strong form market efficiency tests are concerned with whether any information, publicly available or private can be used to generate abnormal returns.
- We generally take it for granted that insiders are capable of generating higher than normal returns on their transactions.
- There is even some evidence that insiders are able to generate abnormal returns on apparently legal transactions that are duly registered with the SEC.
- Jaffee examined SEC insider transaction filings and determined that stock performance relative to the market after months when insider purchases exceed insider sales. When insiders sell, shares that they sold are outperformed by the market.
- Why do insiders appear to outperform the market on their duly registered insider transactions? Are insiders trading on the basis of their private information or do they actually have superior trading ability?
- Givoly and Palmon [1985] suggest that transactions generating these superior returns are not related to subsequent corporate events or announcements.

  — They found that insider superior returns were not explained by the published announcements.
  — This may suggest that these insiders may either simply have superior investing ability or may generate higher returns for

themselves on the basis of information that is not later announced.

— On the other hand, perhaps insiders are trading on the basis of insider information that is not subsequently released on a specific date.

- Managers are not obliged to announce most types of inside information according to any particular schedule. In addition, many insiders participate in plans to regularly buy (without liability, as per SEC Rule 10b5-1) or sell shares.
- Managers can obtain 10b5-1 protection for trades if they create the plan at a time when they do not have non-public information and they announce their transactions schedule in advance.
- For example, Kenneth Lay was said to have protected $100 million in his own wealth by selling shares of Enron stock through a 10b5-1 plan.
- In addition, insiders always have the right to abstain from trading on the basis of inside information. Thus, it is not illegal to *not buy* shares on the basis of inside information. How would investigators determine whether one declined to trade solely on the basis of inside information?
- Jagolinzer [2005] found that insider trading within the 10b5-1 plans outperforms the market by 5.6% over a 6-month period.
- Insider Returns.

Anomalous Efficiency and Prediction Markets

- The Challenger Space Shuttle Disaster.
- On January 28, 1986, at 11:38 am Eastern Standard Time, the space shuttle Challenger was launched in Florida and exploded 74 seconds later 10 miles above ground.
- The stock market reacted within minutes of the event, with investors dumping shares the four major contractors contributing to building and launching the Challenger: Rockwell International, builder of the shuttle and its main engines, Lockheed, manager of the ground support, Martin Marietta, manufacturer of the vessel's

external fuel tank and Morton Thiokol, builder of the solid-fuel booster rocket.

- Less than a half-hour after the disaster, Rockwell's stock price had declined 6%, Lockheed 5%, Martin Marietta 3% and Morton Thiokol had stopped trading because of the flood of sell orders.
- By the end of trading for the day, the first three companies' share prices closed down 3% from their open prices, representing a slight recovery from their initial reactions. However, Morton Thiokol stock resumed trading and continued to decline, finishing the day almost 12% down from its open price.
- Many months after the disaster, Richard Feynman demonstrated that brittle O-rings caused the explosion. Morton had used the O-rings in its construction of the booster rockets, which failed and leaked explosive fumes when the launch temperatures were less than could be tolerated by the O-rings.
- Yet, there were no announcements of such failures on the dates of the disaster or even within weeks of the explosion. Nonetheless, the market had reacted within minutes of the disaster as though Morton Thiokol would be held responsible.
- In their study of this event, Maloney and Mulherin [2003] found no evidence that Morton Thiokol corporate officers and other insiders sold shares on the date of the disaster.

Prediction Markets

- Price discovery is one of the most important functions of trading, particularly in more transparent markets such as the NYSE.
- Consider the 1988–2008 presidential elections, where an increasing number of online betting markets offered tradable securities on election outcomes.
- The most visible of these markets have been www.intrade.com and www.biz.uiowa.edu/iem/index.cfm
- They trade contracts that pay $1 if a given candidate is elected, which prices less than $1. Thus, if a contract sells for $0.50, one might guess that the market believes that the candidate has a 50% chance of getting elected.

- Security markets are excellent aggregators of information.
- Security prices have been used for many years to estimate a variety of types of probability distributions.
  - Currency traders have used futures prices to estimate future currency exchange rates.
  - Commodity traders have used commodity futures prices to predict commodity prices.
  - Call options are used to estimate implied volatilities for underlying stocks.
  - Implied correlations between two underlying variables such as exchange rates using derivative contracts written on each underlying currency as well as contracts written on both currencies.

- Prediction markets, even with respect to political wagering did not originate with Intrade and the Iowa Electronic Markets. The Curb Exchange (the precursor to the American Stock Exchange) operated wagering markets for presidential markets during much of the late 19th century.
- Such wagering frequently involved large sums of money, with daily volume that often exceeded presidential campaign budgets.
- More recent prediction markets have been quite successful, including the North American Derivatives Exchange (Nadex), a CFTC-registered futures exchange that got its start as HedgeStreet prediction market.
- Presidential Election Winner.

Science, the Government and Prediction Markets

- Is the information provided by markets of use to decision-making entities in business and government?
- Consider an example from the 1990s where, CERN, the European laboratory for particle physics, needed to estimate whether the probability of discovering the Higgs boson was sufficiently high to justify extending the operation of its collider. Traders at the

Foresight Exchange Website (http://www.ideosphere.com/) took positions on whether the Higgs boson would be discovered by 2005, setting a contract price of 0.77 as of 2001.

- We close this section with a few rhetorical questions: Should markets provide information aggregation services to the public? If so, at what cost to traders? Consider the following excerpt from Looney [2003]:

  The Defense Advanced Research Projects Agency (DARPA) was born in the uncertain days after the Soviets launched Sputnik in 1958. Its mission was to become an engine of technological change that would bridge the gap between fundamental discoveries and their military use [Bray, 2003]. Over the last five decades, the Agency has efficiently gone about its business in relative obscurity, in many cases not getting as much credit as it deserved. The Agency first developed the model for the internet as well as stealth technology. More recently, DARPA innovations have spanned a wide array of technologies. To name a couple: computers that correct a user's mistakes or fix themselves when they malfunction and new stimulants to keep soldiers awake and alert for seven consecutive days...

  Then, in late July, the Agency backed off a plan to set up a kind of futures market (Policy Analysis Market or PAM) that would allow investors to earn profits by betting on the likelihood of such events as regime changes in the Middle East. Critics, mainly politicians and op-ed writers, attacked the futures project on the grounds that it was unethical and in bad taste to accept wagers on the fate of foreign leaders and the likelihood of terrorist attacks. The project was canceled a day after it was announced. Its head, retired Admiral John Poindexter, has resigned.

- Poindexter's resignation followed the creation of a contract by Tradesports.com that would pay $100 if he resigned.
- Can markets trading terrorism-based contracts aid in the prediction of terrorism strikes and dealing with the effects of such strikes? If so, should such contracts be traded?

Epilogue

- In his presidential address to the American Finance Association, Richard Roll [1988] discussed the ability of academics to explain financial phenomena:

  The maturity of a science is often gauged by its success in predicting important phenomena. Astronomy, the oldest science, is able to predict the positions of planets and the reappearance of comets with a high degree of accuracy... The immaturity of our science [finance] is illustrated by the conspicuous lack of predictive content about some of its most intensely interesting phenomena, particularly changes in asset prices. General stock price movements are notoriously unpredictable and financial economists have even developed a coherent theory (the theory of efficient markets) to explain why they should be unpredictable.

LECTURE 10

TRADING GONE WRONG

A. Illegal Insider Trading

- Unfair capital markets fail to draw capital.
- Illegal insider trading is traditionally defined as the execution of transactions on the basis of material non-public information.
- Several statutes are generally relied upon to enforce prohibitions on insider trading.

  — Section 10(b) of the Securities Exchange Act of 1934 prohibits employment "in connection with the purchase or sale of any security registered on a national securities exchange or any security not so registered, any manipulative or deceptive device or contrivance in contravention of such rules and regulations as the Commission may prescribe as necessary or appropriate in the public interest or for the protection of investors."

  — Securities and Exchange Commission (SEC) Rule 10b-5 prohibits "any act, practice, or course of business which operates or would operate as a fraud or deceit upon any person, in connection with the purchase or sale of any security."

  — These rules are extended to identify elements of Section 10(b) or Rule 10b-5 insider trading claim:

    - Possession of material non-public information;
    - Trading while in possession of that non-public information;
    - Violation of a relationship of trust and confidence.

171

— Section 14 of the Securities Exchange Act and Rule 14e-3 impose a "disclose or abstain from trading" obligation on any person who trades in securities that will be sought or are being sought in a tender offer, while that person is in possession of material non-public information that he knows or has reason to know has been acquired directly or indirectly from the offer or, the subject corporation. The Securities Exchange Act of 1934 (Section 14e) provided the initial federal statutory insider trading restrictions, though a 1909 Supreme Court decision in *Strong v. Repide* interpreted inside trading by corporate officials without appropriately revealing that information to be a form of fraud.

— A 1980 Supreme Court decision (*Chiarella v. United States*) defined an insider as one who maintains a "relationship of trust and confidence with shareholders."

— The Insider Trading Sanctions Act of 1984 authorized penalties for illegal insider trading equal to three times the illegally obtained profits plus forfeiture of the profits.

— The Insider Trading and Fraud Act of 1988 was intended to help define exactly what constitutes an insider and to set penalties for illegal insider trading activity.

Notorious Insider Trading Cases

• All of the individuals named in the cases that follow were very successful in their businesses, and in most cases, quite wealthy.

• William Duer was appointed Assistant Secretary of the Treasury in 1789 under Alexander Hamilton. Duer used information and connections obtained in his official position, along with substantial leverage to speculate in new US debts and various bank stock issues. His speculation and subsequent failure was a major cause of the Panic of 1792.

• In 1985, Dennis Levine, an M&A specialist was Managing Director at Drexel Burnham Lambert. One of his trading account brokers, a Bahamian subsidiary of a Swiss bank began "piggy backing" off his trades as did the bank's account executive at Merrill Lynch. Merrill Lynch became suspicious of these trades and notified the SEC. Levine implicated fellow M&A specialist Martin Siegel and Ivan Boesky, to whom he had passed illegal trading tips.

- Boesky, considered the leading expert on merger arbitrage, had been paying Levine a percentage of his trading profits gained from Levine's tips. Boesky agreed to a plea, whereby he implicated Michael Milken and Drexel Burnham, along with his friend, John A. Mulheren Jr., the former head of Jamie Securities.

- The investigation into the relationship between Boesky and Milken uncovered a $5.3 million payment in 1986 to Drexel that Boesky had characterized as a consulting fee. A significant amount of other evidence of insider trading was uncovered, but the bulk of the SEC's weak case against Milken and Drexel would be based on the testimony of Levine, Boesky and other convicted felons. The SEC began to focus on Milken's brother Lowell, who might have played a minor role in the insider trading activities, and other relatives including their 92-year-old grandfather. Milken agreed to a plea arrangement. A codefendant of Milken, Alan Rosenthal, took his case to trial, whereby it was tossed by the judge before going to jury, lending significant credibility to the argument that the case against Milken was weak.

- Levine received a 2 year sentence, was fined $362,000, disgorged of $11.5 million in illegal trading profits and paid an additional $2 million in back taxes. Boesky served 2 years in prison, paid $100 million in fines and was barred from the securities business for life. Milken received a 10-year sentence for fraud and illegal market manipulation, which was later reduced to 24 months, fined $600 million and made restitution payments. Milken and other Drexel employees paid $1.3 billion into a pool to settle hundreds of lawsuits. Drexel was ultimately bankrupted in the aftermath of the scandal, fines, loss of reputation and the collapse of the junk bond market.

- Picture from Boesky case.

More Notorious Insider Trading Cases

- Martha Stewart sold approximately 3,928 shares of ImClone, which had just learned that its new prescription drug would not obtain FDA approval. After learning about the drug's setback, Sam Waskal, CEO of ImClone quickly sold shares of his ImClone stock. His broker, Peter Bacanovic, who also served as Martha Stewart's broker, apparently notified her that Waskal was selling shares of his company's stock. The SEC investigated Bacanovic and Waskal, who were ultimately imprisoned. Whether Stewart had engaged in illegal insider trading was not known at this point, and still is not completely clear. Even if Ms. Stewart had been completely forthright about the information that she had received and why she sold the shares, the SEC's case against her would have been weak at best. Ms. Stewart conspired with Bacanovic to fabricate a story about a stop order at $60, leading to charges of conspiracy, obstruction of an agency proceeding and making false statements to federal investigators. She was convicted and sentenced in 2004 to serve 5 months in federal prison followed by five months of incarceration in her Bedford home and 2 years period of supervised release. She also paid a fine and disgorged the reduction in short-term trading losses that she avoided.

- After she was charged in the alleged insider trading incident involving ImClone, but before the general public knew of the investigation, Ms. Stewart sold shares of her own company, Marta Stewart Living Omnimedia, Inc. This exposed her to additional insider trading charges. She was charged for manipulating the price of her company's stock. These charges did not result in convictions.

- In 2011, Raj Rajaratnam, billionaire and founder of the defunct hedge fund, the Galleon Group, began serving an 11-year sentence in the Federal Prison system after being convicted on 14 counts of conspiracy and fraud. This is the longest sentence ever imposed for illegal insider trading. Mr. Rajaratnam was also fined $92.8 million and faced civil and other actions. Mr. Rajaratnam had been accused of having taken more than $50 million in insider trading gains based on tips provided by fellow conspirators at

Goldman Sachs, McKinsey & Co., Intel, Google, etc. Among those implicated in the investigations were Roomy Khan (Intel), Anil Kumar (McKinsey), Danielle Chiesi (Bear Stearns), Zvi Goffer (Galleon), Rajat Gupta (McKinsey and Goldman Sachs), Robert Moffatt (IBM).

- Two interesting facets of this case were the large number of co-conspirators (49, more or less) and the use by authorities of wire and tapes to record conversations, including more than 40 wiretapped phone conversations between Mr. Rajaratnam and his accomplices.

Monitoring Inside Trading Activity

- Successful insider trading prosecutions usually require cooperation from codefendants or damaging information concerning other illegal behavior (such as tax evasion).
- There have been recent improvements to enforcement efforts.
- Surveillance techniques have improved significantly. The SEC, all of the major markets and companies themselves are purchasing software systems to monitor illicit activity.
- The SEC is making use of more resources to monitor insider activity, including formation of special surveillance teams, wiretapping and bounty payments to informants.
- The SEC currently contends with roughly 700,000 tips per year from informants.
- Markets such as the New York Stock Exchange (NYSE), NASDAQ and Chicago Board Options Exchange (CBOE) are making greater use of technology to monitor trading activity for suspicious activities.
- Financial Industry Regulatory Authority (FINRA) has been using an intelligent surveillance application known as the Securities Observation, News Analysis and Regulation (SONAR) system to detect suspicious patterns. Regardless, insider trading enforcement remains difficult.
- Smarts screen.

B. Front Running and Late Trading

- *Front-running* occurs when a broker uses his knowledge of a large pending order to buy (sell) the relevant security in front of the pending buy (sell) order so as to benefit from the market reaction to the large order.
- In one front-running scandal, the US Attorney's Office and the SEC accused brokers from Merrill Lynch of allowing certain clients to listen to conversations involving other clients through broadcasts on Merrill Lynch internal speaker systems. In this "Squawk Box Scandal," some clients were privy in advance to other clients' trades.
- A similar, often legal, but frequently unethical practice is *tailgating*, a form of parasitic trading where the broker places an order immediately after the client's order.
- Another type of ethically questionable parasitic order is *penny-jumping*, where the broker places a buy (sell) order one uptick above (downtick below) the client's buy (sell) limit order, expecting to benefit either from the market's reaction to the client order or to limit his losses by transacting with the client. For example, if the client were to place a large buy order at $50.00, the broker would penny jump by placing her buy order at $50.01. The broker's order will execute ahead of the client's order due to price priority. If the client's order then executes, the broker will profit from any favorable price reaction due to the client's large buy order. If the price declines, the broker can quickly sell his shares to the client at a $0.01 loss.
- Low-latency front running.

C. Bluffing, Spoofing and Market Manipulation

- *Bluffing* is the act of fooling other traders into making unwise trades by convincing them that the bluffer has superior material information about security values.

  — There are a number of ways that traders bluff, both legal and illegal. A trader can bluff the market by placing a bid or offer at a price or in a quantity that exaggerates his or her own true position, interest or lack of interest in a security. For example, a bluffer might place a particularly attractive offer for a small quantity of shares, intending then to sell a much larger quantity of shares after a positive price response to the initial offer.

— As long as such orders are executed, they are usually perfectly legal.

— Bluffers may also simply spread rumors or false information about the value of a company's shares. Such false rumor spreading can represent deceit or fraud, illegal when used to manipulate markets, and perhaps otherwise as well.

- *Spoofing* is the act of placing a quote that is intended to be canceled prior to its execution. Spoofing might be considered a form of bluffing where the trader places a trade that she has no intent to execute.

- Motivations behind spoofing:

  — to overload the quotation system of a market, inhibiting its ability to execute trades;

  — to delay a specific trader's trade execution by placing that trader's quotes behind a series of quotes with higher priority

  — to create the appearance of false market depth or direction, particularly by submitting then later cancelling multiple bids or offers. This type of spoofing is often referred to as *layering*. Layering is frequently accomplished through an high-frequency trading (HFT) program designed to submit many quotations that are canceled after an executed transaction.

- Orders, modifications and cancellations are not considered to be spoofing if they were submitted as part of a legitimate, good-faith attempt to execute a trade.

- In 2001, the SEC alleged that Alexander Pomper submitted a phantom limit order on NASDAQ to purchase 300 shares of the thinly-traded Gumtech International ("GUMM") at $11.375.

  — This limit order improved the NBBO bid by $.3125 from $11.0625, while the NBBO offer was $11.4375 per share.

  — Pomper improved the bid for GUMM, but with a bid that he apparently did not actually intend to fill.

— Then, Pomper placed an order to sell 2,000 shares of GUMM at $11.375 per share through another market making firm. Pomper's sell order was immediately executed at $11.375 per share because the best bid at $11.375 seemed to suggest a higher value and more liquid market for GUMM.

— However, after executing its sell order, Pomper canceled his order to buy GUMM for $11.375, realizing a profit of $625 (2,000 × [$11.375 − 11.0625]) relative to the initial bid for $11.0625.

— In 2002, the SEC announced a settlement with Pomper, whereby Pomper agreed to pay $9,800 in disgorgement and prejudgment interest and $15,000 civil penalty.
Spoofing

Wash Sales

- *Wash sales* are sham transactions intended to create the appearance of sales where, in effect, no sales actually take place.
- The SEC defines a wash sale as a transaction that involves no change in beneficial ownership.
- Wash sales may be intended to manipulate security prices (e.g. conspirators execute transactions with one another to create records of sales prices to deceive other participants in the market).
- A series of wash sales at ever-increasing prices, known as a *jitney game*, can give other investors the impression that the value of the security is rising, leading investors to purchase the stock.
- Wash sales may also involve the sale of securities for tax purposes with offsetting transactions to repurchase the securities or related instruments. The Internal Revenue Service (IRS) defines a wash sale to be a sale and a repurchase of the same security within 30 days. This sort of wash sale is not illegal, though any capital losses and associated tax write-offs generated by this activity will be disallowed by the IRS.
Wash Trading

Other Quote Abuses

- *Quote matching* occurs when a small trader places a quote one tick from that of a large trader so as to profit from the large trader's transaction price pressure, or to use the large trader as a counterparty should prices reverse. Quote matching exploits the option associated with a limit order.
- *Quote stuffing* is the placement of large numbers of rapid-fire stock orders, with most or all of which being canceled almost immediately, frequently for the purpose of clogging trading HFT and other algorithms and data computations. The purpose of quote stuffing is not to execute orders, but to sabotage algorithms of other traders.
- Some dealers post quotes that are very distant from any reasonable market price for the security (e.g. bid for $0.01 or offer at $100,000), not intending or expecting that these quotes would ever be executed. However, in a one-sided market, these *"stub quotes"* quotes might be executed against as liquidity dries up, causing securities to trade at absurd prices.
- Stub Quotes
- Quote Stuffing

Fat Fingers Trades

- In 2005, a novice trader in a subsidiary of Mizuho Financial Group, attempted to sell one share of J-com stock on the Tokyo Stock Exchange for ¥ 610,000 ($5,041).

  — By accident, he transmitted an offer to sell 610,000 shares at ¥ 1 each. In effect, he attempted to sell $3.075 billion worth of stock for $5,041.
  — These 610,000 shares that he attempted to sell represented 41 times the total number of J-com shares issued by the Japanese recruitment company.
  — Mizuho attempted to cancel and reverse the order, but not quickly enough, such that this incident (losses exceeding ¥ 27 billion) wiped out Mizuho's entire profit for the quarter.

— The absence of filters either at the bank or at the Tokyo Stock Exchange to prevent such an obviously erroneous trade played havoc with the market for J-com stock, and caused the entire Nikkei-225 to drop by 1.72%.

— The broader market reaction was largely in response to traders attempting to guess which firm had made the mistake, driving down share prices for nearly all Japanese financial institutions.

— Later litigation assessed a significant portion of the blame on the Tokyo Stock Exchange, and Mizuho recouped some of its losses.

- A trader at Bear Stearns caused a 100-point drop in the Dow after inadvertently entering a $4 billion sell instead of his intended $4 million buy order.

- Morgan Stanley made a similar mistake with a 2004 order for $10.8 billion rather than the intended $10.8 million.

- Washington Post Co. dropped by 99% in less than one second on June 16, 2010 on NYSE Arca and Progress Energy Inc. increased by 90% in less than one second on September 27, 2010 on NASDAQ.

- Nikkei 225 futures contracts dropped by 1.1% on June 1, 2010 as a result of an unintentional algo-order placed on the Osaka Stock Exchange.

- Each of these occurrences illustrates the need (and failures) for effective trade filters, even in the absence of automatic algo executions.

- Fat Finger Buy.

The Flash Crash

- On May 6, 2010, the "Flash Crash," often been blamed on High Frequency Trading, caused the Dow Jones Industrial Average to drop almost 1,000 points in less than 30 min before recovering almost as quickly.

  — Trades were executed at absurd prices, ranging from less than one cent to over $100,000.

  — Exchanges ultimately canceled over 20,000 executions.

— An SEC report noted that the crash was preceded by a rapid algo-initiated short, reportedly by mutual fund group Waddell & Reed (not an HFT), of a \$4.1 billion block of E-Mini Standard & Poor's 500 futures contracts on the Chicago Mercantile Exchange.
— However, HFT firms apparently were counterparties to these shorts, and immediately covered themselves by further shorting (turning the contracts into hot potatoes), drying up liquidity in these markets.
— Within 20 min of the start of the "crash," trading in the E-mini contract was halted for 5 sec, which allowed the market to recover.
— When contract trading resumed, prices quickly recovered most of their losses.
— An important lesson from this and other mini flash crashes is that high trading volume and market liquidity are not the same, especially when hot potato volume is involved.
- 2010 E-Mini Flash Crash

Hot Potato Volume

- *Hot potato trading*: Repeated passing of inventory imbalances among dealers seems to actually dilute the information content of trading.
- This type of trading tends to be more common in the presence of HFTs and where interdealer volume is high.

A Textbook for \$23,698,655.93 (Plus \$3.99 Shipping)

- Consider Peter Lawrence's 1992 developmental biology textbook, *The Making of a Fly: The Genetics of Animal Design*.
  — Michael Eisen, an evolutionary biologist at the University of California reported that he sent one of his post-docs to purchase a copy on Amazon.com
  — Amazon listed 17 copies for sale: 15 used from \$35.54, and 2 new from \$1,730,045.91 (+\$3.99 shipping). The two new copies were offered by two booksellers, Profnath and Bordeebook.

— Their prices quickly increased from over $1.7 million to $2.8 million, and by the end of the day, to $3,536,675.57. Ultimately, the book's price topped out at $23,698,655.93, plus shipping.

- How did this price manage to evolve to over $23 million?

  — Profnath used an algorithm to undercut Bordeebook's price, at 0.9983 times Bordeebook's.
  — Bordeebook used its algorithm that would set its own price at 1.270589 times Pronath's.

- Such algo programs gone bad are not confined to markets for books, and they are not one-time isolated events.
- Hansen Transmissions (HSNTF.PK) manufactures and supplies wind turbine gearboxes. On January 23, 2009, its stock price increased from $1.62, the prior close, to $143.32 on the trading of 100,000 shares, apparently on the news of an alternative energy speech given by President Obama. The next day, trading opened at $1.69. While this scenario itself was not a major market calamity, it does warn of potential meltdowns (e.g. the May 6, 2010 "flash crash") or other market disruptions that might occur with unfiltered or even filtered algo trading.

Buy, Lie and Sell High

- "Pump and dump" schemes occur when the market manipulator touts company's stock with false and misleading statements in the marketplace, causing the stock's price to rise before selling his own shares at inflated prices.
- Spam operations have been linked to pump and dump operations, where operators tout shares of stock and then sell them. Frieder and Zittrain claim that stock volume for touted shares increases dramatically after spam is delivered.
- Frieder and Zittrain found that on days prior to touting, and on days touting takes place, returns are positive. Returns after touting are negative. Two-day returns average –5.25%, worsening further when the intensity of touting increases. Surely no reader of these results would consider purchasing stock on the basis of unsolicited spam. Yet, someone must be. Who? Why? And why does this

buying behavior continue to persist even after transaction returns are so consistently poor?

- Jonathan Lebed, the stock touter described in the previous paragraph, was a 15-year-old trader from Cedar Grove, New Jersey. In September 2000, the SEC settled 11 cases of stock market fraud against this high school student that had resulted in gains ranging from $12,000 to $74,000 from September 1999 to February 2000. With interest, the SEC disgorged $285,000 in illegal profits. With his AOL connection and hundreds of Yahoo Finance postings under numerous fictitious names, Jonathan had apparently purchased shares in small companies and then posted numerous buy recommendations under fictitious names, increasing share volume from 60,000 to over a million per day in the affected companies. He also maintained a website, stock-dogs.com, where he published his opinions and recommendations. It was reported that Jonathan's father, Greg Lebed had a heart attack and other heart issues during the period of Jonathan's trading and SEC battles. However, the ending of this story was not all bad for Lebed. In his settlement with the SEC, Lebed was permitted to keep over $800,000 in profits from other transactions. Mr. Lebed remains an active trader and distributes a newsletter, available online through http://lebed.biz.
- Pump and Dump

Banging the Close

- The CFTC defines *banging the close* as a "manipulative or disruptive trading practice whereby a trader buys or sells a large number of futures contracts during the closing period of a futures contract (that is, the period during which the futures settlement price is determined) in order to benefit an even larger position in an option, swap, or other derivative that is cash settled based on the futures settlement price on that day."
- Consider the case involving Amaranth Advisors, LLC, which incurred a lose of $6.4 billion in the early Spring of 2006. The fund's failure arose from losses in trading highly leveraged natural gas contracts on New York Mercantile Exchange (NYMEX).

- The Commodity Futures Trading Commission (CFTC) later charged Amaranth and its former head trader, Brian Hunter, with trying to manipulate natural gas futures prices.
- More specifically, Hunter was accused of banging the close, flooding the then open outcry NYMEX futures markets with "series of rapid and successive" orders for natural gas during the final minutes of trading before the close, thereby forcing prices down in this less active market as buying interest diminished. The actual intent of his selling activity, according to the CFTC, was to depress natural gas prices in the ICE, where Amaranth held much larger short positions through swap contracts.

Closing Price Manipulation

D. Rogue Trading and Rogue Traders

- Rogue trading is systematic unauthorized trading, trading with unapproved counterparties or trading with unapproved products. In rogue trading, normally traders exceedingly risk limits and/or loss limits and is accompanied by efforts to conceal unauthorized actions.
- Nick Leeson, chief derivatives trader at Barings' Singapore office, single-handedly brought down the centuries-old Barings Bank.

  — What are the lessons to be learned from Leeson's fraud?
  — The bank failed to sufficiently segregate trading and back office (record-keeping) functions.
  — Management did not react appropriately when it was warned of increased concentration of financial risks from a relatively small trading unit.
  — Continued trading fraud, at least initially, is often committed not for personal gain, but to cover poor performance or losses.
  — Incentive-based compensation contributes to trading fraud, not only motivating the perpetrator, but his supervisors as well.
  — A single rogue trader can bring down even the largest and most venerable of financial institutions.

— The superstar trader should merit the closest observation, not only to assure that his trading is legitimate, but to understand the secrets to his success.

E. Trading and Ponzi Schemes

- Ponzi schemes are not trading schemes. However, Ponzi schemes have been used by rogue traders to mask illegal or unprofitable trading activity.
- In 2007, one of the most respected members of the Wall Street community, Bernard Madoff revealed to his son that his investment firm, Madoff Securities was a Ponzi scheme.

  — This meant that Madoff lost or pocketed clients' money, and when asked or forced to meet client obligations, used funds raised from other clients to meet these obligations.
  — Madoff pleaded guilty to 11 counts of securities fraud on March 12, 2009.
  — Previously, Madoff had maintained a highly successful trading and market-making business, accounting for as much of 12% of NASDAQ volume.
  — He was an active securities market regulator, having served on the NASD and NASDAQ boards during much of the 1980s, and had even served in 1990–1991 as Chairman of the Board of NASDAQ.
  — Madoff accepted large sums of money from "feeder funds" such as Walter Noel's Fairfield Greenwich Group, Tremont Capital, Stanley Chais and Avellino and Bienis as well as banks such as Santander.
  — Madoff regularly provided statements and trade confirmations to clients, apparently almost entirely fabricated. He claimed to be engaging in a trading practice known as "split strike conversion," a simple collar strategy involving the S&P 100. Madoff claimed to take long positions in a basket of stocks resembling the S&P 100, purchased S&P Index 100 puts while writing S&P calls. In a Black–Scholes framework, his strategy should have produced a return comparable to the riskless rate,

much less than the 14–20% that he actually "paid" to most of his investors.

— David Friehling, whose tiny accounting firm Friehling & Horowitzin in Rockland County New York audited Madoff's records, was paid approximately $12,000–$15,000 per month (after 2004), was also charged with securities fraud.

REVISION AND EXAM PREPARATION

■ Regulation + Revision

- Regulation of stock markets in Australia
- Institutions/regulated markets
- Why should markets be regulated?
- Data requirements for regulation

■ Regulatory Bodies

- Australian Regulatory Institutions
- The Australian Securities Investment Commission (ASIC) regulates companies, both listed and unlisted
- ASIC both creates regulations for listed companies as well as enforces these regulations. In some countries (i.e. Canada + US), these functions are separated
- This enforcement requires real-time stock market surveillance for prohibited conducts
- The Australian Prudential Regulation Authority (APRA) regulates banks and insurance firms, ensuring they have sufficient reserves, etc.

■ Why should markets be regulated?

- Regulators have a mandate to ensure markets are both "fair and efficient"

- It is important to make sure that all participants in regulated markets have equal access to information, and that no participants have systematic advantages
- Conducts like insider trading, front running, etc. allow some participants to profit at the expense of others
- This is detrimental to the investor's confidence and participation in a "healthy" capital market

■ Mandate for the Regulators

- Generally there are two components of a regulator's job:
  — Ensure markets are fair
  — Ensure markets are efficient

■ But how can we evaluate "fair" and "efficient"?

- Measuring the Mandate
- Efficiency is easier to measure, generally we want low transaction costs and prices which reflect fundamental value
- Transactions Costs Measures:
  — Effective Spread
  — Quoted Spread
  — Price Impact
  — Amihud Illiquidity
  — Depth of the Orderbook

■ Measuring Efficiency

- Price efficiency can be measured using things like:
  — Volatility of prices (standard deviation)
  — Adherence to a random walk (variance ratio)
  — Delay with which stocks incorporate index-level information
  — Autocorrelation of returns over fine intervals

■ Measuring "Fair"

- Fairness is an ambiguous term. Generally, fairness is interpreted as a "level playing field"
- In reality, we can measure the extent to which participants engage in prohibited conduct
- We could measure data such as:
  — Insider Trading
  — Closing Price Manipulation
  — Broker-client Front-running
  — Spoofing
  — Pump and Dump
  — Wash Trading

■ Data Requirements for Regulation

- Stock market surveillance technology such as SMARTS to regulate
- This software takes all trades and quotes, combines with market events and looks for manipulative conduct
- ASIC require brokers to provide them with trader IDs on every trade
- This assists in identifying suspicious behavior

■ Recent Regulatory Responses

- Market integrity rules released.
- On August 12, 2013, we released market integrity rules on dark liquidity and high-frequency trading, following extensive internal analysis and consultation with the industry
- These final rules aim to improve the transparency and integrity of crossing systems and strengthen the requirements for market participants to deter market manipulation. The rules will come into force in stages over 9 months
- We have also released guidance on the rules which clarifies ASIC's expectations of market operators and participants, and a report on submissions made on the proposed rules

■ Final Exam Structure

- 3 h + 10 min reading time
- 5 sections (each worth 20 marks)
  - 10 Multiple Choice Questions
  - 2 Parts — Computation + Explanation
    - Trading Question
    - Arbitrage Question
  - 2 Parts — Short Answer
    - Regulation
    - Manipulative Conduct
  - 2 parts — Computation + Explanation
    - Trading/Dark Pools (Computation)
    - Dark Pools (Short Answer) — Information Leakage
  - 2 Parts
    - Facilitation/Agency Trading (Computation)
    - Market Innovations (Short Answer)

■ Section 1

- For the first parts of the course, read the book and work through the exercises, this will prepare you "theoretically" and for the multiple choice questions.

■ Section 2a — Facilitation

- You are about to facilitate a trade for your client who is selling one million shares of BHP Billiton Limited (BHP). The current best bid and ask prices are \$35.78 and \$35.80, respectively. You expect that it will take 5 days to sell the shares if you sell an equal amount each day, starting today. You expect to be able to sell 1/5 of the shares on the first day at an average price equal to the bid price \$35.78. You estimate that BHP shares will decline in value by 1% each day over the next 5 trading days, so that each day your average price for 1/5 of the shares will be 1% lower. Your client requires an upfront payment for this order. In order to earn half a percent (on the total value traded) for facilitating the trade, what price will you pay your client? Show all your work.

■ Section 2b — Trading

- It is 30 min before the closing of the trading day on September 24, 2015, and you are about to execute an options strategy for your client. Your client wants exposure to the upside of 1,000 Google Inc. (GOOGL) shares. Your client assumes that GOOGL will not fall from the current level of more than $50 and is likely to increase significantly. Base your strategy on the provided prices, using ask price for purchases and bid price for sales.
- Suggest a strategy that has a zero capital outlay and provides an exposure to a larger move on the upside in GOOGL. You can use several different option contracts, they can be puts and calls, you may purchase or write, you may use different expiry dates.
- Show your recommended strategy as a payoff diagram and explain when the strategy returns a profit and when it returns a loss.
- Suggest a trading plan for how to enter this strategy.
- (Stock and Option quotes in GOOGL at the time of the trade are presented below.)

■ Section 2c — Data

■ Section 3a — Manipulative Trading

- Choose one of the following manipulative conducts and provide the following:
  - A definition
  - An example of the conduct
  - Why would someone engage in such conduct?
  - What impacts might it have on the markets?
  - How could such conduct be discouraged through regulation?

- Insider Trading, Closing Price Manipulation, Spoofing, Pump and Dump/Hype and Dump, Wash Trading, Front Running

■ Section 3b — Regulation

- Define regulatory bodies in Australia
- Which markets do they regulate?
- Why should we regulate markets?
- What kinds of things should be prohibited?

■ Section 4a — Dark Pools + Transaction Costs
■ Section 4b — Dark Pools

- Discuss the different financial innovations which have been implemented for dark pools
- How can information be disseminated from dark pools to traders?
- What innovations could assist in minimizing such information revelation?

■ Section 5 — Market Innovations

- Discuss why a market would introduce a speed bump
- How will speed bumps impact the market? Pay particular attention to
  - Impact on liquidity suppliers
  - Impact on fill rates and measures of spreads
  - Impact on rest of the market
  - Why would participants be willing to pay more for the ability to cancel orders without experiencing a speed bump?

PART 2

ADVANCED APPLICATION AND RESEARCH

LINKING MARKET MICROSTRUCTURE TO MAINSTREAM FINANCE

TRADING MECHANISMS, MARKET REGULATION AND INSIDER TRADING

Advanced Market Microstructure

1. Trading Stories Harris Chapter 2
2. Hasbrouck Chapters 1 and 2 Introduction and Trading Mechanisms
3. Connecting to Corporate Finance: Insider Trading: Regulation and Empirical Research
4. Discussing a Research Paper

Trading Stories from L. Harris *Trading and Exchanges*, Chapter 2

Trading

- Reading Time...
- A retail trade in an NYSE listed stock: Figure 2.1.
- A retail trade in a NASDAQ stock: Figure 2.2.
- An institutional trade in an NYSE stock: Table 2.1.
- An institutional trade in a NASDAQ stock: Figure 2.3.
- A very large block stock trade

Application to ASX:

- A retail trade in an ASX stock:
  - Submitted online or over phone to broker who routes the order to the Trade Match (NASDAQ OMX technology) for execution in the limit order book at the best available sell or buy order.
- An institutional trade in an ASX stock:
  - May be submitted over phone to institutional broker or directly to market *via* brokers system.
  - Crossed, facilitated or submitted in parts using an algorithmic order-submission system.
  - Order-crossing systems set up by specialized brokers (dark pools were introduced by most brokers, but now practically shut down by regulators). Some early players are still active in Liquidnet and Australian version of Posit, ITG Markets.
  - http://www.asic.gov.au/asic/asic.nsf/byheadline/13-213MR+ ASIC+makes+rules+on+dark+liquidity%2C+high-frequency +trading?openDocument.
  - ASX CENTERPOINT replaced the fragmented dark pools from 2011.

Trading stories at home

Examples of typical trading situations

- The portfolio manager of an institution Super Fund Plc wishes to increase the weight of Newcrest Mining (ASX: NCM) — one of the largest gold mining stocks — in their portfolio by 3% as the gold price has started to rise. The institution is currently holding 1 million shares worth AU$12.3 million.

  - Solution
  1. The Super Fund's trader James would pull up the online access system IRESS they have through one of the many brokerage firms they use for their investments to see what the current situation in NCM is, he sees: (OVERLEAF).
  2. At 3 pm in the afternoon, 1,989 shares at AU$12.36 and 3,838 at AU$12.37.

3. James quickly estimates that they need to purchase 0.03×1 million $= 30,000$ shares of NCM. At the moment, the depth at the best offer price is only 1,989 shares!

4. James calls up one of the institutional investment banks (say UBS) they use to find out what is the best they can offer 10,000 shares of NCM at.

5. James also calls his contact at Macquarie Bank and asks them to put in an order for 30,000 shares of NCM into the Australian Stock Exchange dark pool, Center Point.

Why? What is James trying to achieve? Why doesn't he buy what is available in the market, about 5,000 shares? Why does he ask for 10,000 shares only? Why two brokers? What is a dark pool?

Discussion of institutional trade superfund pic

— Why?
— What is James trying to achieve?

  — Minimize the market impact of his relatively large order (compare to daily volume of AU$25 million in total).

— Why doesn't he buy what is available in the market, about 5,000 shares?

  — James decides it is not wise to directly start buying from the market as this may temporarily lead to higher prices for the some of the stocks he is trying to buy.

— Why does he ask for 10,000 shares only from UBS?

  — James does not wish to expose his full interest to one broker as this may provide him with a better price, as UBS does not see how much he really needs (remember these tactics may have negative impact on the relationship between broker and customer if misused).

— Why two brokers?

  — It is always good to have several brokers competing for your business to maximize price improvement.

Quote for NCM

NCM $19.300 -$0.01 (-0.05%)

NEWCREST MINING FPO

Add to Watchlist | Add to Alerts | Manage Orders   Buy   Sell

Share Quote

Discuss in Community

Bid ($)	Offer ($)	High ($)	Low ($)	Volume	Trades	Value ($)	Open ($)	Previous Close ($)
19.290	19.380	19.540	19.210	3,238,143	12,898	62,669,707	19.210	19.310

Market Depth

View: **Price Detail** | Order Detail

Buyers

No.	Volume	Price ($)
1	1,000	19.290
1	1,000	19.280
1	1,500	19.230
2	300	19.200
2	2,000	19.190
2	600	19.150
1	50	19.100
1	600	19.090
1	200	19.070
2	2,000	19.060

92 buyers for 77,915 units

Sellers

Price ($)	Volume	No.
19.380	2,797	1
19.470	1,000	1
19.490	499	1
19.500	400	1
19.520	2,000	2
19.540	509	1
19.580	500	1
19.600	46,895	4
19.610	5,000	1
19.660	1,035	1

174 sellers for 252,497 units

Date Range: 1d | 5d | 1m | **1y** | 5y

22.50
20.00
17.50

Volume   5M   0M

Jan   Apr   Jul   Oct

Share Details

52 Week High ($)	24.270
52 Week Low ($)	18.575
Last Traded	11/10/2018 4:10:14 PM
Trading Status	Inquiry
Market Status	Inquiry
Margin Lending LVR	70%

Market Indices

Index	Value	Change
All Ordinaries	5,993.483	-170.320
ASX SPI 200	5,835.000	10.000

— What is a dark pool?

    — One of the latest options in trading venues is to route orders to a dark pool where orders can be executed with less exposure to other traders, and hence may receive price improvements as compared with the "lit" main ASX market where all orders are visible pre-trade.

Market microstructure topics

Harris chapter 1, "trading stories"

- Most important lesson from trading stories: the difference between the methods used to execute a small retail trade vs. a large institutional trade!
- Table 2-1 Summary of trades for an institution from Harris, p. 19.

Table 12.1: Summary of Bob's Trades

SHARES	PRICE	NOTES
48,000	39.84	POSIT
200,000	39.87	Morgan Stanley block trade
20,000	39.88	Merrill Lynch floor trades
32,000	39.90	Merrill Lynch floor trades
28,000	39.95	Merrill Lynch floor trades
72,000	40.00	Meirrill Lynch trades with book
400,000		

- In Australia: Broker has a choice of where to route an order:

    — Algorithmic execution, disposed the order gradually following a pre-programed strategy.

    — Centerpoint (anonymous pool for large institutional trades) executes orders at the mid-point when there is demand and supply available.

    — Negotiate the trade over the phone and do an off-market trade (at mid-point or price outside the spread) in large enough order.

    — Route the order to the public market ASX Match.

Introduction to Market Microstructure and Trading Mechanisms

Hasbrouck Chapter 1

Market microstructure topics

- Sources of Value and Reasons for Trade
  - Common and private components of value
    - Cashflow
    - Investment horizon, risk exposure, tax situation, etc.
  - *How can we measure these? (see, e.g. Hendershott et al. research)*
  - *Are these the same as public (corporate announcement) and private (inside) information?*
- Trading mechanisms
  - Microstructure analysis is typically very specific about the details of the trading mechanism, limit order book/hybrid, visible limit order book, one consolidated or several (fragmented) platforms/orderbooks?
- One or many prices?
  - A market clearing price rarely occurs in real-world markets, e.g. bid, ask prices
- Liquidity
  - Elasticity in price
  - Cost of trading
  - Dynamic attributes: executing over a short horizon more costly than patient trade-off?
  - Depth breadth and resiliency
  - Suppliers and demanders of liquidity
    - Sell side vs. buy side
    - Agents offering option to trade vs. agents who trade spontaneously active vs. passive
    - Today's markets, the supply of liquidity is a strategic choice that can be quickly reversed!

— Externality: consolidation vs. fragmentation
— The number of participants in the market for each security depends on features of the security high market cap, index component widely held, etc.

   — exo vs. endogenous attributes.

— The sources and origins of liquidity is what market microstructure is about!
— "Liquidity is created through a process in which counterparties reveal information in exchange for knowledge ultimately leading to trade" (paraphrased from ICor Brokerage website)
— Transparency

   — Pre-post trade, order information vs. broker or trader identity

— Econometric issues
— Market microstructure data is:

   — Distinctive, classified as: point processes
   — Well ordered
   — Large
   — Short in time span. Should you use calendar time or trade time?

Questions

Open questions and potential research topics:

- What are optimal trading strategies for typical trading problems?
- Exactly how is information impounded in price?
- How do we enhance the information aggregation process?
- How do we avoid market failures?
- What sort of trading arrangements maximize efficiency?
- What is the trade-off between fairness and efficiency?
- How is market structure related to the valuation of securities?
- What can market/trading data tell us about the informational environment of the firm?
- What can market/trading data tell us about long-term risk?

Hasbrouck Chapter 2

Trading mechanisms: Current institutional details in global markets

— Limit order markets

  — Direction, quantity and acceptable price
  — Unexecuted orders, "the book"
  — Multiple of consolidated limit order book
  — Priority rules, price then time, obvious? Not across books, sometimes volume gets priority
  — Market orders walking the book
  — TIF, IOC and AON orders
  — Hidden orders
  — Iceberg orders
  — Modeling trade: Accurate data but rarely possible to map orders submitted and canceled by the same trader. Exceptions? Depository data sets, terminal ID information.

— Floor Markets

  — NYSE, US Futures Exchanges, Frankfurt, example: bund future DTB vs. LIFFE.
  — Financial institutions that rely heavily on electronic markets have large trading floors for diverse markets.
  — For example, pricing of a corporate bond and all its related sources of information, e.g. government bonds, swaps and interest rate futures benefit from proximity.
  — No longer necessary to realize (in a single market) economies of scale. This may be achieved across multiple markets.

— Dealers

  — Dealer markets: customer relationships, direction of order flow.
  — Dealers in hybrid markets: dealers can make markets work here, they might otherwise fail.
  — Market making in derivative and other complex instruments, foreign exchange.

- New results on the consolidation of the Australian market due to new regulations of dark pools. CMCRC MQ, Financial Inte.
- Traded value migrated from ASX darkpool to main market and to a lesser extent from Chi-X dark pool to Chi-X main market.
- Effective spreads fell significantly on ASX and to lesser extent on Chi-X.
- No effect on price discovery.
- No effect on market depth.

- Auctions and other clearing mechanisms

  - Coordination of trade, a single price clearing

- Bargaining

  - In economic terms, security trading is an ultimatum game.

Connecting to Corporate Finance: Insider: Regulation and Emperical Research

Regulation of securities markets

Market regulation

- Regulators create and enforce rules that facilitate trading.
- How academic (and industry) research is often drawn upon making policy recommendation.
- Areas of regulation: continuous disclosure, corporate reporting, market manipulation, insider trading (our focus is here).

  - Discussion papers circulated within industry participants
  - Academic researchers commissioned (neutral and unbiased?)
  - Survey of research in the literature
  - Own research by regulators such as ASIC and APRA
  - Self regulation: first-hand responsibility with ASX and Chi-X. Regulate listed firms and brokers (market makers)
  - Regulatory Capture: examples
  - Lobbying: examples
  - MiFID I and II

Regulation of insider trading

— In limelight due to high publicity for breaches
— Prosecutions in Australian equities markets at historical high: statistics
— High profile cases in the AUD currency markets
— Talk about limited resources for regulation and enforcement
— Law only effective if enforced

Empirical Research into Insider Trading

Connecting market microstructure to mainstream finance

Insider trading is a central topic under corporate governance, also under market microstructure due to the empirical nature of the research.

First session: Market regulation, corporate governance and insider trading

- Discussion of the connection between corporate finance and market microstructure — regulation of market, corporate governance
- Insider Trading
- Berkman *et al.* (2015), inside the director network: when insiders trade outside stocks. Under reveiw by *Review of Financial Studies.*

Empirical research on insider trading

Key papers and findings

- US evidence: Jaffe (1974), Lakonishok and Lee (2001), Rozeff and Zaman (1988, 1998), Seyhun (1986) and Ravina and Sapienza (2010).
- UK evidence: Fidrmuc *et al.* (2006).
- International: Clacher *et al.* (2009) discuss the results of insider trading studies in several other countries.
- Main finding: "It is well known that members of corporate boards earn significant abnormal returns when they buy their company's own stock as insiders."

Current Research by our team

— Berkman *et al.* (2014), published in *Journal of Finance*.
— Berkman *et al.* (2015), inside the director network: when insiders trade outside stocks. Under reveiw by *Review of Financial Studies*.

   — Class discussion: Paper presentation

— Centre for International Financial Regulation (CIFR), ASIC supported and CIFR-funded investigation of insider trading in Australia.

   — Impact on uninformed traders
   — Do better connected directors benefit more from being insiders?

Discussing academic research

Analysis and discussion template

- In addition to some theory from textbook chapters, we will mainly focus on analysis of academic research papers.
- Typical layout, title page with abstract, introduction with paper layout plan, literature review if applicable, theory if applicable, institutional detail of investigated market if applicable, data description and methodology, reporting of results and detailed analysis, conclusions with a more general analysis and conclusion, plus suggestions for future research.
- How do you best tackle a paper that can at first glance seem difficult and technical with complicated equations?

1. Make your own summary of the study, starting with a thorough read of abstract and introduction, highlighting and making notes of key points.
2. Try to determine the research question, aim of paper and where it fits in the big picture.
3. Assess the theory and methodology at the best of your ability without getting stuck in the equations, they are usually presented

in a very compact form in a paper, sometimes extensions are provided in an abstract.

4. Find and list weaknesses in argument, theory, methodology, data and analysis.
5. Propose constructive criticism and suggestions for improvement and further analysis.
6. Develop your own topic (a primer more about this later when we are skilled at analyzing papers).

— See a suggestion for seven steps of the research process from Cornell University: http://olinuris.library.cornell.edu/ref/research/skill1.htm

Discussion: Berkman *et al.* (2015), Inside the Director Network: When Insiders Trade Outside Stocks

What next, future research topics

Dealer markets vs. limit order markets

- For next time read prior to class.
- Pagano and Roell (1996), "Transparency and liquidity: A comparison of auction and dealer markets with informed trading", *Journal of Finance*.
- Goettler *et al.* (2005), Equilibrium in a Dynamic Limit Order Market, *Journal of Finance*.
- Copies will be available on Blackboard (you may in future download copies of assigned published research papers in advance through the university library website).

"WORKSHOP" and revision questions

Questions for thought

- What do sell-side and buy-side traders have in common? How do they differ? Do you expect much labor mobility between these two types of traders?
- How might competition between regulatory agencies benefit the economy? What effect do you expect it would have on innovation in trading products and trading procedures?

- Should congress consolidate SEC and the CTTC into a single regulatory agency? How about consolidating ASIC and APRA in Australia?
- Why do traders, brokers and exchanges generally welcome regulation? When do they oppose it?
- How should regulators decide issues?
- Who should appoint regulators?
- How did the US regulation that every order must be executed at the NBBO create an opportunity for the emergence of high-frequency traders?

LECTURE 13

LIMIT ORDER MARKETS

Order driven markets

Introduction

— Order-driven markets use trading rules to arrange their trades: oral auctions, single-price auctions, continuous-electronic auctions and crossing networks.
— Oral Auctions

    — Order precedence rules

        — Price, time, public order — decimalization lowered effect of precedence

    — The trade pricing rule — oral auctions "discriminatory"

    — Trading floors, pits and posts

— Rule-based Order-matching Systems

    — Examples:
    same order flow in Single price auction vs. Continuous auctions.

The Uniform-Pricing Rule and Single-Price Auctions

— Definition of the measure of trader surpluses — the difference between trade price and the buyers $(-)$ or sellers $(+)$ valuation of the security Should be positive and maximized!

— Discriminatory pricing rule preferred by large traders that can break up orders
— Uniform pricing rule preferred by limit orders — rather see all traders get same price than a market where large traders discriminate among traders
— *Table 6-4 with order flow*
— *Tables 6-5 and 6-6 with supply and demand schedule*
— *Table 6-7 with trader surplus in the single (uniform) price auction example*

The Discriminatory-Pricing Rule and Continuous Two-Sided Auctions

— *Table 6-8 with trades in the continuous auction example*
— *Table 6-8 with trader surpluses in the continuous auction example*

The Derivative Pricing Rule and Crossing Networks

- Real world examples: POSIT Instinet and NYSE after hours of trading session I websites

  — NYSE.com article: more than 40 crossing networks "Dark Pools". Alternative Trading Systems (ATS), Trade Report Facilities (TRF), Electronic Communication Network (ECN).
  — Australia at least 12 dark pools, now replaced by Center Point ASX and Center Point Chi-X.

- Price ownership
- Problems with derivative pricing

  — Stale prices and well-informed traders
  — Price manipulation
  — High frequency traders trying to front-run orders.

Summary and Points to Remember

— Limit order favor the uniform pricing rule.
— Large market order traders prefer the discriminatory trade-pricing rule.

— Price priority is self enforcing, but secondary precedence rules are not.
— Secondary precedence rules require a large minimum price increment to be economically significant.
— Single price auctions maximize trader surplus.
— Continuous auctions generate more volume for a given order flow.
— Markets that use the derivative pricing rule are subject to price manipulation.

GPR(2005) Discussion Paper Limit Order Books

Journal of Finance (2005): Goettler et al.

- Equilibrium in Dynamic Limit Order Market (definitions)

  — In traditional models based on Kyle (1985) or Glosten and Milgrom (1985), prices are set by an intermediary. Prices are equal to the expected value of the asset (conditional on public information and signed transactions) plus spreads to compensate the dealer.
  — By contrast in a limit order market, prices are determined by strategic traders, and need bear no such relationship to the value of the asset.
  — Previous attempts to model dynamic limit order markets have made assumptions to obtain analytical solutions.
  — This paper generates artificial data with the purpose of simulating a market where true asset values are known, to consider relations between quoted spreads, transaction prices and consensus value in a market that closely resembles real world limit order books.

GPR(2005) Methodology and Model

Equilibrium in dynamic limit order market

- How do they do this?
- Model: infinite horizon version of Parlour (1995) discrete time model of a pure limit order book market.

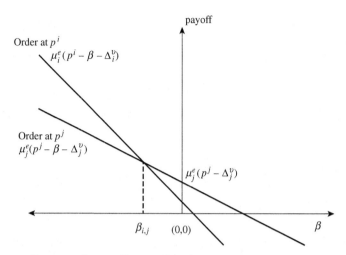

Figure 2.   Expected payoff to sell orders at different prices. The figure denotes the expected payoff to a seller from sell orders at prices p^i and p^j, where $p^i > p^j$. Here, μ_i^e is the seller's belief that a limit sell submitted at price p^i will eventually execute, β is his private value, and Δ_i^v is his expectation about the change in common value before the share executes. The notation for an order at price p^j is similar. The X-axis has the seller's β, and the Y-axis the expected payoff.

- Discuss the existence of a Markow-perfect equilibrium in this game and present an algorithm for numerically finding such an equilibrium.

- Base Case: chose parameter values that qualitatively capture salient market features and still have computational tractability.

- Artificial data: once an equilibrium is found, beliefs are fixed and a further 500,000 trader arrivals are simulated. Trade-off between limit and market orders is considered. For a given book, trader strategies at thresholds when traders are indifferent between two actions are represented. Figures 2 and 3 show that equilibrium order submission has similar properties in this simulation.

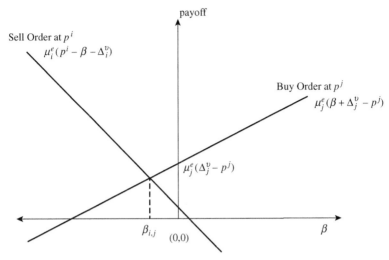

Figure 3. Payoff to sell order at price p^i and buy order at price p^j.
This figure denotes the expected payoff to a seller from a limit sell at price p^i and
a limit buy at price p^j. Here, μ_i^e is the seller's belief that a limit sell submitted at
price p^i will eventually execute, β is his private value, and Δ_i^v is his expectation
about the change in common value before the share executes. The notation for
an order at price p^j is similar. The X-axis has the seller's β, and the Y-axis the
expected payoff.

GPR(2005) Simulation of model

Sell order

The trader chooses the optimal price at which to submit his sell
order. He can submit a market sell at the bid price B, or a limit
sell at any higher price. Denote the trader's belief about execution
probability for an order placed at price p^i as $\mu_i^e = \mu_t^e(k, i, L_t, X_t)$.
Similarly, denote $\Delta_i^v = \Delta_t^v(k, i, L_t, X_t)$. The trader submits a sell
order at price p^i if

$$\mu_i^e(p^i - \beta - \Delta_i^v) \geq \max_{j \neq i} \mu_j^e(p^j - \beta - \Delta_j^v). \tag{9}$$

For a market order, $\mu_i^e = 1$ and $\Delta_i^v = 0$.

Sell and buy order

GPR(2005) Results

- VA Transaction costs and welfare — Trader (consumer) surplus
- VE The mid-point as a proxy for consensus value — frequently incorrect 25.9%
- VI Example of Policy Evaluation: Effect of Tick Size — Market + Limit − Total + 2.1%
- Conclusions

  — Paper introduces a class of models that embody features of existing markets
  — Explicit calculation of trader surpluses is a major contribution
  — Determine implications of endogenous order submission for relations:

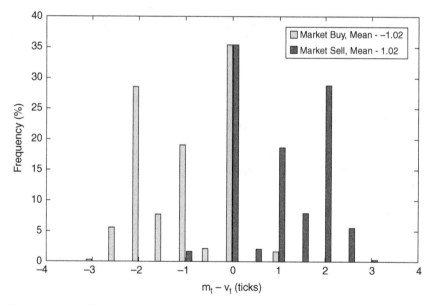

Figure 10. Histogram of midpoint minus true value, conditional on trade. This figure provides a histogram of the difference between the midpoint of the bid-ask spread and the consensus value of the asset, conditional on a transaction occurring in that period. The transaction involves either a market buy order or a market sell order.

Table XII: Difference in Ticks between Midpoint and Consensus Value, and Transaction Price and Consensus Value, Conditional on a Market Sell Order

For the three models considered, the table shows the average difference between the midpoint of the bid-ask spread (m_t) and the consensus value (v_t), and the average difference between the transaction price (p_t) and the consensus value (v_t). These averages are computed only for periods in which a market sell order was submitted.

Model	$m_t - v_t$	$p_t - v_t$
Base case	1.02	0.10
Zero volatility	0.62	−0.19
Immediate cancellation	0.99	0.02

— Transaction prices, transaction costs, trader surplus, effective spreads

— Mid-point on average proxies consensus value, but when trade occurs it is not!
— Effective spread not a good measure of surplus, because supply and demand of liquidity is endogenous. How?

— Can improve model of liquidity demand and supply by including endogenous order flow, to improve accuracy of predicted price impacts of order execution.

E. The Midpoint as a Proxy for the Consensus Value

Future Research Stemming from GPR(2005)

Potential future work

- A theoretical model that fits real markets
- Can be simulated (C code available from Parlour and Rajan)
- My proposal: as I have access to insider trades, use these real world insider trades and noise trades around these to parametrize the model
- Then either simulate a more close to real world case, or
- Use the model framework to analyze the real data

- Problem: How do we determine investors private beliefs about value β and probability of execution x? Can we just assume distributions?
- *GPR has one new paper on the topic in JFE 2009*

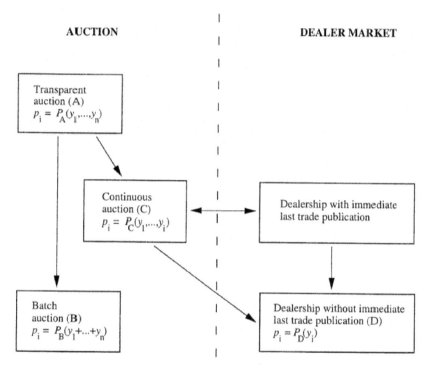

Figure 1. Stylized trading systems, ranked by decreasing transparency. The figure gives a partial ranking of trading systems in terms of their transparency and summarizes price formation in each system. Arrows point in the direction of *decreasing* transparency. Arrows point in both directions when two trading systems have the same degree of transparency. Trading systems not connected by arrows cannot be ranked vis-à-vis each other. For each market, the price p_i for the i-th order coming to the market ($i = 1, \ldots, n$) is determined as a function (P_A to P_D) of the order flow information available to those who price it, where y_i denotes the (signed) size of the i-th order. The index i of the order is assumed to convey no information about the identity of the trader who placed it. The arguments of the pricing functions P_A to P_D indicate exactly what information is available in each of the markets A to D when the price is formed.

Pagano and Roell (1996)

A comparison of Auction and Dealer Markets with Informed Trading

- Theoretical, experimental, focus market transparency
- A realistic model
- Description of markets
- A. transparent auction (Treasury bond issues, privatizations, house sales)
- B. Batch auction (opening call auction ASX, SGX, Euronext)
- C. Continuous auction (NYSE-Euronext, ASX, Chi-X)
- D. Dealership (NASDAQ, LSE, Treasury Bond Markets), now all with alternative limit order book platforms hybrid markets, for example, London Stock Exchange: SETS and SETSQX: *"From our premium fully electronic order-driven services for liquid UK and international Global Depositary Receipts, through to our quote driven market maker services for less liquid securities, our Trading Services are designed to maximize liquidity in the securities traded on them."*

The following result then obtains:[10]

Theorem 1: *Comparison of Transparent Auction and Dealer Markets, with Exogenous Informed Trader Strategy. Assume that:*

A. *there is one insider who knows the final value of the security, v, where $v \sim G(v)$, and m uninformed traders who trade $u_l, \ldots, u_m$, independently drawn from $F(\cdot)$;*

B. *both $G(v)$ and $F(u)$ are symmetric distributions about $\bar{v}$ and 0 respectively;*

C. *the insider's trading strategy $\tilde{X}(v)$ is the same in both types of market and satisfies assumption X.*

Then the expected transaction cost to uninformed traders is lower in the transparent auction than in the dealership market, for all trade sizes.

The continuous auction, harder to analyze pp. 590–591:

We now turn to an analysis of a continuous auction. We can conceive of a continuous auction market as one in which potential traders arrive in a random sequence and submit market orders for execution. When the first trader's order is filled, the other orders are not yet known. Upon execution, its size and price are publicly announced, and price quotes are updated. Then the second trader formulates his order, which is filled at a price equal to the best estimate of the security's value, given the size and direction of both the first and the second orders. This process continues until the last order is filled at a price equal to the best estimate of the security's value given all the orders.

The security's value is either high (V_H) or low (V_L) with probability 1/2 each, so that its expected value is $\underline{V} = (V_H + V_L)/2$. There are only two potential traders, arriving in random order: a noise trader who either buys or sells a unit of the security (with probability $z/2$ each) and an informed trader who knows the security's true value (with probability q). In pricing the first order, the history of the order flow. But in this simple example that is readily seen to be the case. In both periods, the equilibrium strategy of the informed trader is identical: he buys a unit if he knows that the security is worth V_H, sells it if he knows that it is worth V_L, and does not trade otherwise.[14]

Since a noise trader arrives first or second with equal probability, this argument shows that the expected price he pays is the average of the dealer quote and the expected auction market price. Thus trading costs in the continuous auction are lower than in a dealer market but higher than in the transparent auction.[15]

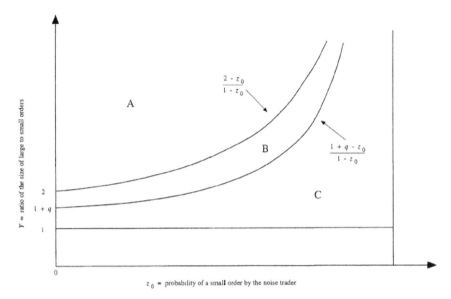

Figure 2. **Insider's strategy and model parameters.** Regions show how the strategy played by the insider in equilibrium depends on the relative probabilities of small and large noise trades and on their relative sizes. In region A, the insider only places large orders in both auction and dealer markets. In region B, he adopts a mixed strategy only in the auction market, while in region C he mixes in both.

Endogenous insider trading without pre-commitment to a strategy: The case of different trade sizes (large and small)

Future Research from Pagano and Roell (1996)

A relevant framework for analyzing todays markets:

wrgs to transparency and liquidity

D. Summary

In *all* the models examined in this section, greater transparency reduces, or at least does not increase, the *average* trading costs of noise traders. In all the cases that we have examined, the result that transparency enhances market liquidity still holds when the insider's strategy is treated as endogenous. It is still an open question whether this conclusion can be extended to as general a setting as that of Theorem 1, where almost no restrictions are placed on the distribution of insider information and noise trades.

However, our results are weaker than those obtained when the insider's strategy is held constant across trading systems. While greater transparency tends to lower average trading costs for noise traders, it may not do so for all trade sizes.

- New Textbook Foucault *et al.*, 2013, *Market Liquidity*, Oxford, Oxford University Press.
- *Rent extraction and lobbying*, p. 297. Consider why markets today are so opaque despite the results showing that transparency is generally good for market welfare.
- Pham, T.P. and Westerholm, J. 2015, "A survey of research into broker identity and limit order book transparency", *Australasian Accounting Business and Finance Journal*, Vol. 9.

LIQUIDITY PROVIDERS: DEALING AND MARKET MAKING

Liquidity Suppliers: Dealers, Market Makers and Their Inventories

- Liquidity providers
  - Liquidity providers exist in many forms:
    - Dealers and market makers,
    - Block traders,
    - Value traders — the ultimate suppliers of liquidity,
    - Arbitrageurs,
    - Buy-side traders — depending on the order submission strategy,
    - What type of speculators may also provide liquidity?

Dealers

- Introduction:
  - *Merchants who make money buying low and selling high.*
  - *Dealers generally provide additional liquidity to the markets through their activities and are rewarded for this activity by potential trading profits.*

— *The liquidity dealers provide is generally in the form of immediacy as they allow for impatient traders to transact small to average volume quickly at reasonable prices without having to search out other traders with the opposite interest.*

- Trading with dealers
- Attracting order flow
- Dealer quotation decisions
- Dealer inventories
- Inventory risk

  — Diversfiable
  — Adverse selection
  — Market values vs. fundamental values

Industry Examples

- *How Madoff Controlled Adverse Selection*
- *Why Do Foreign Exchange Markets Trade Incredible Volumes?*

Additional Material

Liquidity providers around the world

- Equities exchanges — see the following table.
- Very few futures markets have obligated market makers, but most options markets rely on market makers to provide liquidity.
- Foreign Exchange: <50% of volume rest in online-based broker markets.
- Bond markets: mostly traded through dealers (who may provide online limit order books to their clients); some bonds are exchange traded.

Resarch Paper Westerholm

LOB / Hybrid Dealer / Dealers with Affirmative Obligations 2006

Exchange	Relative Tick Size	LOB Market	Hybrid Dealer Market	Stocks with Affirm. Deal.	Delayed Rep. Blocks	Brk ID Disclosure	Iceberg Orders	Levels Ordr Book Displ.	GDP per capita	Share Hold Protection	Institut. Brk Fee	Comp. Listed	Population	Trading US Time
1 Amsterdam	0.00071	0	0	0.67135	0	0	1	5	23,100	2	0.0013	387	15,735,000	2.0
2 Australia	0.00442	1	0	0	0.06598	1	1	15	22,200	4	0.0023	1287	18,705,000	0.0
3 Brussels	0.00386	0	0	0.92242	0	0.712551	1	5	23,900	3	0.0011	268	10,152,000	1.9
4 Budapest	0.00182	0	1	0	1	1	0	5	7,800	2	0.0048	62	10,076,000	1.0
5 Frankfurt	0.00054	0	1	1	1	1	1	15	22,700	3	0.0012	851	82,178,000	4.5
6 Germany	0.00124	1	0	0.87781	1	0.001044	1	15	22,700	3	0.0012	851	82,178,000	1.5
7 Helsinki	0.00326	1	0	0	0	1	0	5	21,000	3	0.0014	150	5,165,000	1.5
8 Hong Kong	0.00841	1	0	0	1	1	0	5	23,100	5	0.0016	708	6,801,000	0.0
9 Jakarta	0.10753	1	0	0	1	1	0	15	2,800	3	0.0046	276	209,255,000	0.0
10 Johannesburg	0.00437	1	0	0	0	1	0	10	6,900	5	0.0026	668	39,900,000	0.5
11 Korea	0.00226	1	0	0	0	1	0	10	13,300	3.353	0.0034	712	46,480,000	0.0
12 Lima	0.01406	0	0	0	0	0	0	15	4,400	4	0.0050	239	25,230,000	6.5
13 London	0.00099	0	1	0.24004	1	0	0	15	21,800	5	0.0014	2274	58,744,000	2.0
14 Luxembourg	0.00064	0	0	0	1	1	1	15	34,200	2	0.0011	277	426,000	2.0
15 Milan	0.00149	0	1	1	0	1	0.98573	1	21,400	5	0.0010	217	57,343,000	2.0
16 Nasdaq	0.00151	0	1	0	0	0	1	1	33,900	5	0.0012	4829	276,218,000	6.5
17 India	0.00101	0	0	1	0	1	0	1	1,800	5	0.0048	700	998,056,000	0.0
18 New York	0.00091	0	0	0	0	1	1	1	33,900	5	0.0012	3025	276,218,000	6.5
19 New Zealand	0.01022	1	0	0	0	1	1	5	17,400	4	0.0008	172	3,828,000	0.0
20 Osaka	0.00178	1	0	0	0	1	0	3	23,400	4	0.0008	1281	126,505,000	0.0
21 Oslo	0.00362	1	0	0	0	1	0	5	25,100	4	0.0013	215	4,442,000	0.5
22 Paris	0.00087	0	0	0.67774	1	0.666677	1	5	23,300	3	0.0014	487	58,886,000	2.0
23 Sao Paulo	0.00075	0	1	0	0	1	1	15	6,150	5	0.0026	399	167,988,000	5.5
24 Singapore	0.01718	1	0	0	1	0	1	15	27,800	4	0.0019	493	3,522,000	0.0
25 Bangkok	0.00717	1	0	0	0	1	1	3	6,400	2	0.0050	392	60,856,000	0.0
26 Shanghai	0.00093	1	0	0	0	1	0	3	3,800	4	0.0013	819	1,266,838,000	0.0
27 Shenzhen	0.00100	1	0	0	0	1	0	3	3,800	4	0.0013	551	1,266,838,000	0.0
28 Stockholm	0.00426	1	0	0	0	0	1	15	20,700	3	0.0014	300	8,892,000	4.5
29 Switzerland	0.00142	1	0	0	0	0	1	1	27,100	2	0.0020	412	7,344,000	2.0
30 Tel-Aviv	0.02634	1	0	0	1	1	0	1	18,300	5	0.0032	654	6,101,000	0.0
31 Toronto	0.00086	1	0	0	1	1	0	15	23,300	5	0.0025	1456	30,857,000	6.5
32 Tokyo	0.00176	1	0	0	0	0	0	3	23,400	4	0.0008	1935	126,505,000	0.0
33 Warsaw	0.00386	1	0	0	0	1	1	5	7,200	5	0.0050	221	38,740,000	0.5

Two Important Exchanges

- New York Stock Exchange:

  — A specialist is the designated intermediary that operates as both a broker and a dealer.
  — Each stock is assigned to one specialist firm that has affirmative obligation to make a fair and orderly market.

- NASDAQ:

  — Over 500 member firms act as market makers.
  — Use their own resources to represent a stock and compete with each other to buy and sell.

- Now over 50 competing ATS

Why Market Makers

- Market makers or dealers are important to provide liquidity to the other market participants.
- Exchange designated market makers need to "insure fair and orderly markets by buying and selling from their own inventories, trading in a stabilizing manner against public order, and taking on the corresponding inventory risk."
- This is especially important during high market volatility period.
- Market makers are compensated for this obligation by giving special access to order information, presence on the trading floor, discounts on exchanges fees or rebates for providing liquidity, and sometimes paid by listed companies.

DMM (Former Specialists)

- NYSE and Frankfurt as well as CBOE equity options market, AMEX ETF markets, still employ a system where exchange members are lisensed as designated market makers. These specialists must continuously quote two-sided markets in the shares/options they specialize in.
- Most specialists are dual traders.

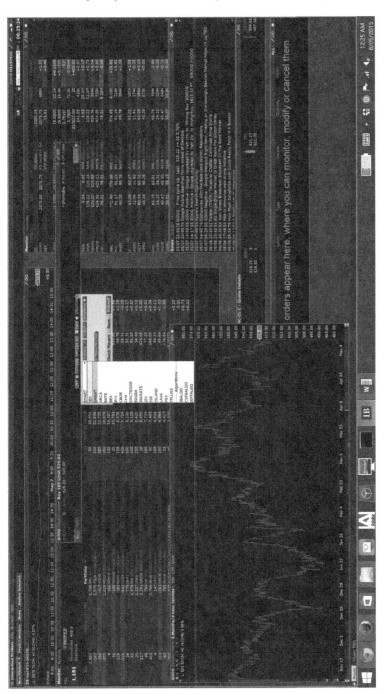

US MARKET OPEN May 7, 2015

- Two sets of regulations, affirmative obligations (specialists must provide liquidity when there isn't from public) and negative obligations (specialists cannot trade on his own account when there is enough liquidity on the market) regulate when specialists must trade and when they must not.
- These obligations may become costly, since specialists are obligated to provide liquidity when it is the most costly and refrained from demanding liquidity.
- These costs must be compensated for by privileges granted by the exchange that make specialist activity profitable.

Responsibilities

- Fair and orderly markets, continuous price path, provide a maximum spread buy and sell price for a minimum amount of shares (100).

Privileges

- Information about order flow, the right to make decisions after other traders, the ability to create the market quote, look-back timing options, collect commission from system order flow
- Most important: access to information about orders

Profit strategies: Harris (2003)

— Speculative strategies — price prediction using information about order flow
— Quote-matching strategies — lower risk using order imbalance information
— Cream-skimming strategies — choosing to trade with less informed traders
— Gunning against stop orders

— Stopping stock and the look-back timing option
— Conducting the market open
— Receiving brokerage commissions for orders routing through exchange and for working orders from the floor.

The Future

The future of designated market makers

— **NYSE**: Crack down on specialist activities.
— Change of management and development toward a more automated trading system.
— Public can access an "Open Book System" (priced for professionals).
— DMMs have less privileges, same affirmative obligations.
— **Frankfurt**: The specialist market is more liquid, while the nationwide electronic market Xetra also has market makers (not specialists). Different (larger) stocks trade on Frankfurt, more foreign investors cross listings.
— **Amex**: Specialists in more complex instruments like exchange traded funds and derivatives may have an important function in the future as price setters; often trade with voluntary market-making firms who only trade for profit and have no affirmative obligations.

NYSE Market Model as of 2014

"Unique Market Model: Only NYSE and NYSE MKT equities markets offer a unique combination of high-tech automation for low latency and complete anonymity as well as high-touch participation by market professionals for orderly opens and closes, lower volatility, deeper liquidity and price improvement opportunities throughout the trading day."

COMPARISON OF SPECIALIST VS. DMM

	Specialist (Old)	DMM (New)
Trading Responsibility	Agency responsibility, visibility to all incoming orders	Market maker with quoting obligation, no advanced "look"
Priority	Yield on all orders	Parity
Obligartions	Affirmative and negative obligations, open, close	Affirmative obligations, open, close
Technology	S-quotes, SAPI	Addition of Capital Commitment Schedule (CCS)
Economics	Economic incentive	Economic incentive tied to providing liquidity

Risk Exposure for Dealer

- Inventory holding costs: the costs associated with carrying non-zero inventory
- Adverse selection costs: costs associated with trading with informed traders
- Order processing costs: not very significant in today's automated markets with electronic depository receipts

Dealer Traded with Informed Trader

Suspected condition	Tactic	Purpose
Sold to a well-informed trader	Raise ask price Lower ask size	Discourage further sales to informed traders.
	Raise bid price Raise bid size	Encourage clients to sell quickly and thereby restore inventory position before prices rise.
	Buy from another traders at his/her ask price	Quickly restore target inventory; this strategy pays for liquidity, but the cost may be less than the loss that will result if prices rise while the dealer is short.
	Buy a correlated instrument	Hedge inventory risk and speculate on information.

(Continued)

Table (*Continued*)		
Bought from a well-informed trader	Lower bid price Lower bid size	Discourage further purchases from informed traders.
	Lower ask price Raise ask size	Encourage clients to buy quickly and thereby restore inventory position from prices fall.
	Sell to another trader at his/her bid price	Quickly restore target inventory; this strategy pays for liquidity, but the cost may be less than the loss that will result if prices drop while the dealer is long.
	Sell a correlated instrument	Hedge inventory risk and speculate on information.

Example of Seller Initiated Trades MSFT

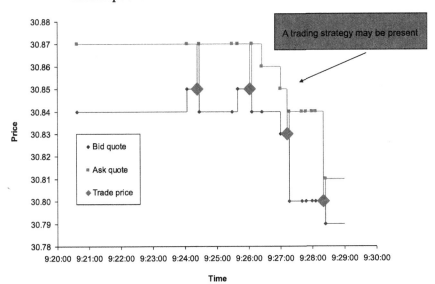

LIQUIDITY, VOLATILITY AND TRANSPARENCY

Assignment

— Preview of tasks.

— Pick one of the research papers in our readings (or suggest another paper of your preference which is broadly in the area of market microstructure).

— Expand, modify or change research question: "Redefine the research question of the paper according to your own preferences and observations. Aim to sharpen the research question, improve or change the hypothesis. Apply the research question to a different market/setting. Tip: apply what we are learning in the book about current market developments and data availability, etc, 20%.

— Propose a suitable methodology for the research task, 20%.

— Propose and define a suitable (empirical) data set to use for this study, data may be local, international, real market, simulated or survey-based, 20%.

— Turnitin will be up and running on Blackboard for assignment hand in with the **due date 29 April (4pm).**
— Full instructions on Blackboard this weekend!

Liquidity

The search for liquidity

— Unilateral searches, you search for a good match, e.g. a good price, and stop when benefit $<=$ cost of searching.
— Bilateral searches

- Passive or active — limit orders vs. block traders
- You may not be able to return to the best match that you have identified during your search. While you continue to search, so does the other side!
- **Liquidity is the object of bilateral search.**

Liquidity dimensions — a source of confusion

1. **Immediacy: How quickly** trades of a **given size** can be arranged at a **given cost**:
Market orders or marketable limit orders

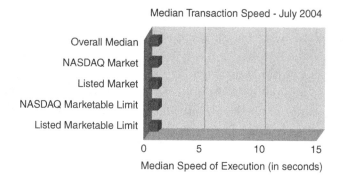

Median Transaction Speed - July 2004

Immediacy: Example: Best Execution Performance of an Online Broker

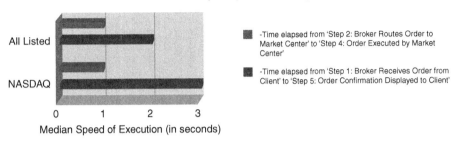

Median Transaction Speed (Market Orders) - July 2004

As a result of computerized trading, executions now occur within a few milliseconds.

Statistics:

Hearing on "Conflicts of Interest, Investor Loss of Confidence, and High Speed Trading in U.S. Stock Markets" (June 17, 2014) (citing statistics that average execution speed has improved by 90% since 2004 — from 7 sec to 0.7 sec today), http://www.hsgac.senate.gov/ subcommittees/investigations/hearings/conflicts-of-interest-investor -loss-ofconfidence-and-high-speed-trading-in-us-stock-markets.

— Liquidity dimensions

2. **Width**: Refers to the **cost of doing a trade** of a **given size.**

   Smaller trades bid–ask spread + brokerage fees and exchanges fees

Width: Example: What Happens When an Exchange Change Transparency

	Pre (−20 to −1 days)	Post (0 to +20 days)	Difference	t-statistic	Post (+21 to +40 days)	Difference	t-statistic
Panel A: Euronext Paris							
Absolute Spread (€)	0.2230	0.1887	−0.0343	−3.61***	0.1760	−0.0471	−4.93***
Relative Spread	0.2817	0.2290	−0.0527	−8.28***	0.2209	−0.0608	−9.6***
Best Bid & Ask Depth	1,863	3,540	1,677	9.73***	4,663	2,800	15.03***
Depth	11,192	16,431	5,239	7.29***	20,492	9,300	12.8***
Volume (000s)	1,010	917	(96)	−1.29	1,030	19	0.23
Return Standard Deviation	0.0236	0.0188	−0.0048	−14.9***	0.0175	−0.006	−18.55**
Panel B: Tokyo Stock Exchange							
Absolute Spread (¥)	5.74	6.28	0.53	2.3	6.07	0.32	1.46
Relative Spread	0.1933	0.1920	−0.0013	−0.48	0.1879	−0.0053	−2.1*
Best Bid & Ask Depth	69,484	57,238	−12,247	2.92**	61,400	−8,084.5	−1.82*
Depth	235,347	185,944	−49,403	−3.79***	21,2363	−22,984	−1.53
Volume (000s)	3,210	3,950	741	3.55***	3,020	−192	−1.2
Return Standard Deviation	0.0065	0.0077	0.001	14.27***	0.0067	0.00019	2.63**
Panel C: Korea Stock Exchange							
Absolute Spread (Won)	328.43	265.97	−62.461	−2.45**	329.12	0.69	0.02
Relative Spread	0.7088	0.62	−0.0888	−5.8***	0.7164	0.008	0.45
Best Bid & Ask Depth	N/A	N/A	—	—	N/A	—	—
Depth	N/A	N/A	—	—	N/A	—	—
Volume (000s)	790	1090	303	7.28***	901	111	3.34***
Return Standard Deviation	0.0338	0.0343	0.0005	1.65*	0.0402	0.006	19.66***

Not to be confused with breadth of ownership:
number of long investors/shares outstanding

$$\text{bid–ask spread} = \text{best ask} - \text{best bid}$$
$$\text{(expressed in dollars/cents)}$$
$$\text{relative bid–ask spread} = \frac{\text{ask} - \text{bid}}{\text{mid point}} = \frac{(\text{ask} - \text{bid})}{(\text{ask} + \text{bid})/2}$$

— Liquidity dimensions

3. **Depth: Size of a trade** that can be arranged at **a given cost**.

    Measured in units available at a given price of liquidity.

— Liquidity dimensions

4. **Resiliency**: How quickly do prices revert to former levels after they change as response to large order flow imbalances initiated by uninformed traders?

    Related to the role of value traders 19.2.4 p. 402 Harris (2003).

Not too much research and established methodology, a potential area of study? Why? Why not?

Suggestion: Could we use the realized spread to measure resiliency?

The graph shows the price development after a typical trade in a limit order book market (Korea).

$$\text{Realized spread (profit by market maker)}$$
$$= \text{Effective spread} - \text{Market impact}$$

More about this under Transparency.

Depth: Market Impact Costs: $\frac{\text{(VWAP} - \text{MIDPOINT)}}{\text{MIDPOINT}}$

	Pre (−20 to −1 days)	Post (0 to +20 days)	Difference	t-statistic	Post (+21 to +40 days)	Difference	t-statistic
Panel A: Euronext Paris							
Parcels of €1,000	0.0028	0.0023	−0.0005	−7.84***	0.0022	−0.0006	−9.23***
Parcels of €10,000	0.0034	0.0027	−0.0007	−6.78***	0.0026	−0.0008	−8.39***
Parcels of €100,000	0.0062	0.005	−0.0012	−7.18***	0.0047	−0.0015	−9.18***
Parcels of €1,000,000	0.0079	0.0066	−0.0013	−9.2***	0.0063	−0.0016	−11.26***
Panel B: Tokyo Stock Exchange							
Parcels of ¥1,000,000	0.0019	0.0019	−4.7E-05	−1.97*	0.0018	−0.0001	−3.37***
Parcels of ¥10,000,000	0.0020	0.0019	−4.E-05	−1.66*	0.0019	−0.0001	−3.66***
Parcels of ¥100,000,000	0.0025	0.0025	0.00004	−1.31	0.0025	−2.1E-05	−0.74
Parcels of ¥1,000,000,000	0.0042	0.0041	−0.0001	−1.82*	0.0041	−0.0002	−2.3**

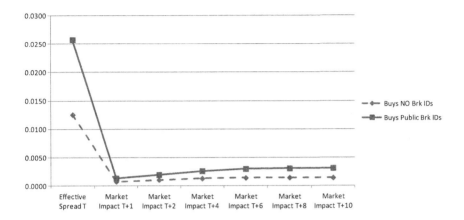

Liquidity providers

— Market Makers

- o **Allow impatient customers to trade** by offering liquidity as quoted bid and ask prices — small size — frequent trades.

— Block Dealers/Upstairs Traders on the ASX

- o Offer liquidity to **"uninformed" clients** who want to **trade large positions** — know their customers well.

— Value Traders

- o Collect as much information about fundamental values as is economically sensible. Trade when prices differ substantially from their estimated values.
- o Prices often change when uninformed traders demand liquidity.
- o Value traders buy underpriced and sell overpriced securities and thus are the **ultimate suppliers of liquidity.**
- o **Make markets resilient**
- o The prices where value traders buy and sell are **the outside spread.**

— Precommited traders

  ○ **Offer liquidity to obtain better prices** using limit orders
  ○ Aggressive, close to the market
  ○ May drive dealers out of the market
  ○ Narrow spreads, little depth
  ○ May turn into liquidity demanders if orders are not executed

— Arbitrageurs

  ○ Arbitrageurs are **porters of liquidity**:
  ○ The price discrepancies between two markets they exploit come about due to demand of liquidity in one market.
  ○ They demand liquidity in the market when best available and supply liquidity in the market where traders demand it.

An Event Study of a Liquidity Changing Event

Example: Westfield Group Stapled Security WDC

— The three Westfield companies were merged to improve the scope and awareness of the security and ultimately its liquidity.
— What if we wanted to investigate if the merger was successful in improving the liquidity of the stock?
— Let us make a quick analysis of WDC.

Event Study Methodology

Immediacy

— Immediacy: straight through processing in electronic automated trading system in combination with average size trades — no problem. Larger trades may have to be negotiated off market and/or executed in Center Point.

Width

— **After: WDC** (new stapled, today) $15.41 - 15.43 = 0.129\%$
  WDC (new stapled, yesterday) $15.33 - 15.35 = 0.130\%$
— **Before: WSF** (Westfield holdings) $12.6 - 12.65 = 0.396\%$

Depth[1]

— **After: WDC** 100 shares: spread 1541 − 1544 → VWAPvMidp
  1,000 shares: spread 1541 − 1545 → VWAPvMidp
  10,000 shares: spread 1541 − 1545 → VWAPvMidp
  100,000 shares: spread 1532 − 1550 → VWAPvMidp **1.17%**

— **Before: WSF**
  10,000 shares: spread 12.69 − 13.00 = **2.41%**
— Note: These calculations need to be done over a number of days
  for both periods so that the results can be statistically tested.
  A difference in difference (DID) approach may be suitable.

Difference in Difference DID Methodology

— Popular methodology from Economics and Medical Science now
  has entered Corporate Finance. May also be good to use for Mar-
  ket Microstructure Events.
— **The faith in "one observation" event studies has faded**.
— May be better to create a well-matched sample of stock, size, price
  industry, which are traded in an alternatively designed market.
— Compare **DID** between the two samples across the event.
— Observations are organized like this:
— Stock Date, Statistic (e.g. spread) Treatment Dummy, Win-
  dow Dummy Interaction Variable Treatment Dummy × Window
  Dummy
— WDC, 20××0105, 0.00396, 1, 0, 0
— WDC, 20××0205, 0.00129, 1, 1, 1
— WS(US), 20××0105, 0.0030, 0, 0, 0
— WS(US), 20××0205, 0.0030, 0, 1, 0

Points to Remember

— Liquidity is the object of a bilateral search problem.

---

[1]Comparison: After the stapling of the securities 100,000 shares could be traded
at "half" the spread compared to 10,000 shares a year before.

— Liquidity is the ability to trade when you want to trade, at low cost.
— Brokers and exchanges organize liquidity that traders offer.
— Liquidity has several related dimensions, often discussed but rarely well understood.
— Market makers primarily supply immediacy.
— Block/upstairs traders primarily supply depth.
— Value traders make markets resilient.

Volatility

Definition: The tendency for prices to change unexpectedly

— Changes through time — Episodic volatility — can be scary, e.g. October 1987, 1998, 9/11 2001, August 2007
— If returns are normally distributed, a crash like 1987 would happen with a probability of 10^{-160} a -27 SD event!
— The 1989 crash was -5 SD event, once every 14,756th year, 1998 and 2001 had similar probability
— The flash crash of May 2010
— Relation: volatility risk and profit
— Concerns option traders
— Concerns regulators

— **Fundamental volatility vs. Transitory Volatility**

  ○ Changes in values vs. trading by uninformed traders

— Fundamental volatility

  ○ Factors: **any factor that determines value**
  ○ Predictability: **Only unexpected events** cause volatility
  ○ Storage costs: **Commodities that are expensive to store** are very sensitive to changes in supply and demand — very volatile prices
  ○ Fundamental uncertainties: For example, stocks in **certain industries**, such as values of technology companies, depend on outcomes of research and success of products that do not yet exist — highly volatile prices

— Transitory volatility:

  ○ **Bid–Ask bounce**: For example, Glosten and Milgrom models which we will discuss next time

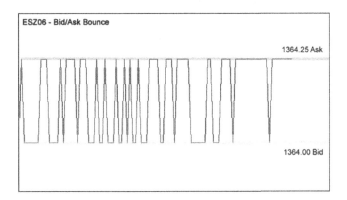

  ○ **Large orders** and cumulative order imbalances
  ○ Transitory volatility is closely related to transaction costs for uninformed traders — **low in liquid markets**
  ○ **Regulators** need to make sure volatility they try to reduce is **transitory NOT fundamental**

— Measuring volatility:

  ○ Total volatility = Fundamental + Transitory volatility
  ○ Measured as variance, standard deviation, means absolute deviation (Parkinson's ln(High/Low) metric), and recently realized volatility.[2]
  ○ Measured as implied volatility from options pricing models (B&S) VIX. Some forecasting ability if comparing short to long future on VIX
  ○ To identify the two components statistical models are necessary. General principle:

   • Fundamental volatility random, not reverting price changes
   • Transitory volatility correlated with order flow and reverting → transitory price changes negatively correlated

---

[2]Squared five minutes intra-day returns.

o An advanced model by Nobel Laureate Robert Engle: ACD models (ARCH GARCH) that models time varying volatility. The latest applications for intra-day volatility forecasting are in this area. (VCE GARCH is apparently the latest)

Forecasting Volatility: GARCH (1,1)

Why forecast volatility?

— The three main purposes of forecasting volatility are for risk management, for asset allocation, and for taking bets on future volatility.

o A large part of risk management is measuring the potential future losses of a portfolio of assets, and in order to measure these potential losses, estimates must be made of future volatilities and correlations.

o In asset allocation, the Markowitz approach of minimizing risk for a given level of expected returns has become a standard approach, and of course an estimate of the variance–covariance matrix is required to measure risk.

o Perhaps, the most challenging application of volatility forecasting, however, is to use it for developing a volatility trading strategy. Option traders often develop their own forecast of volatility, and based on this forecast they compare their estimate for the value of an option with the market price of that option.

— The simplest approach to estimating volatility is to use historical standard deviation, but there is some empirical evidence, which we will discuss later, that this can be improved upon.

— Stylized facts: Squared returns are positively autocorrelated. Volatility not only spikes up during a crisis, but it eventually drops back to approximately the same level of volatility as before the crisis. This is what analysts try to model.

— **GARCH(1,1)** (one period lags) is probably the most widely used application, good to have an idea what this is about!

Nice Graphical Simple Demonstration
https://www.youtube.com/ watch?v=o-Kf6Y419hU
https://www.youtube.com/watch?v=KJbR0nRinD4&ebc=ANyPxK
rsXm5v3M5VgHY0vpkO3F8f7Axv8ARQwWe9e131jsjJpWUl3IY2w
WN2IFJEMl2Keq92VCiik4592CB5u5l-ie_C-Df2tQ

Points to Remember

— Fundamental volatility is due to unexpected changes in fundamental valuation factors.
— Fundamental price changes are correlated with volume when only
a few traders know new information about fundamental values.
When such information is common knowledge, prices can change
on little or no volume.
— Fundamental volatility may be scary, but it is necessary for the
efficient allocation of resources.
— Prices must change as the world changes if they are to reflect all
current information about instrument values.
— Transitory volatility consists of price changes caused when impa-
tient uninformed traders seek liquidity
— Transitory volatility and transaction costs are closely related.
Both are high in illiquid markets.
— The price changes associated with transitory volatility tend to
revert. Price reversion causes negative correlation in a price
change series.
— Transitory volatility is identified by the negative serial correlation
due to price reversals.

Reading Article

Bessembinder, H. *JFQA*, 2003

Trade Execution Costs and Market Quality after Decimalization.
Why is it important?

1.

2.

3.

How to measure Market Quality?

Important Findings?

Ray...

Transparency

— A controversial topic — Rent extraction and competition vs. fairness
— Last weeks reading Pagano and Roell, and their later textbook with Foucault highlight the issues
— Gets little mention in the textbooks.
— Only a few papers have been published in top three journals.

Reading Article (1)

— Boehmer *et al.* (2005)

Lifting the veil: An analysis of pre-trade transparency at the NYSE

— We study pre-trade transparency by looking at the introduction of NYSE's OpenBook service that provides limit-order book information to traders off the exchange floor. We find that traders attempt to manage limit-order exposure. They submit smaller orders and cancel orders faster. Specialists' participation rate and the depth they add to the quote decline. Liquidity increases in that the price impact of orders declines, and we find some improvement in the informational efficiency of prices. These results suggest that an increase in pre-trade transparency affects investors' trading strategies and can improve certain dimensions of market quality.
— What is OpenBook?
— "the information disseminated does not include the specialist's proprietary trading interest or floor broker interest. As a result, the information in OpenBook does not reflect total depth in the market, but rather only depth in the limit-order book."

Reading Article (2)

— Subscribers increased from 2,700 to 4,000 during the first four months after January 24, 2002
— Is it still in use today?

Methodology

— Choose the full two trading weeks prior to the introduction week as the pre-event period.
— For each of the first four months after the introduction of Open-Book, we use the first full weeks of trading: February 4–15, March 4–15, April 1–12 and May 6–17.
— **Findings**

Implications

Reading Article (3)

— Effective spread for orders vs. effective spreads for trades:

  o The data that market centers publicly report to comply with the requirements of the SEC are monthly averages of the measures.
  o Use the SOD files to generate effective spreads for market and marketable limit orders for the pre- and post-event periods. In addition, we follow Rule 11Ac1-5 by putting orders into size categories in terms of the number of shares in an order ([1, 499], [500, 1,999], [2,000, 4,999], [5,000, 9,999], and [10,000, ∞]).
  o To demonstrate the advantage of using the effective spread of orders as a measure of transaction costs, consider the following hypothetical example. Say a marketable buy order for 1,500 shares arrives at the NYSE via the SuperDOT system at 10:15:01 A.M. The quote mid-point at the arrival time is $30.01. The order is executed in two trades: 500 shares at 10:15:03 A.M. for a price of $30.03, and 1,000 shares at 10:15:10 A.M. for a price of $30.05. The quote changes in between these two trades and the new quote mid-point at 10:15:07 A.M. is $30.03. The trade effective spread would have two observations: ¢2 per

share for the 500-share trade and ¢2 per share for the 1,000-share trade. The effective spread for the order, however, is computed against the quote mid-point at the time of arrival, and is weighted by the shares in the orders, so that the effective spread of the order would be $[500 \times (30.03 - 30.01) + 1000 \times (30.05 - 30.01)]/1{,}500 = ¢3.33$.

Additional Reading (3) Also on BB

Pham et al. (2015)

Intra-day revelation of counterparty identity in the world's best-lit market

— We study the impact of post-trade broker identity disclosure on market efficiency, trading volume and bid–ask spreads in a unique South Korean experiment. The Korea exchange market design allows us to compare two sessions within the same trading day, a relatively opaque morning session when the identity of brokers is largely unknown and a transparent afternoon session when the identity of the brokers in the previous session is known. We find that simply revealing the *ex post* order flow of the major brokers to the entire market improves market efficiency and increases trade volume both economically and statistically as asymmetric information is rapidly removed. Realized spreads fall indicating greater competition between market makers and liquidity suppliers, while market impact increases due to more rapid price discovery. These findings support a policy of transparent counterparty identity post-trade.

The Correct Way to Calculate Spreads

— The adding-up property between effective spread, market impact and realized spread

Buy/Sell Init	Trade Effective Sprd T	Trade + 8 Market Impact T + 8	Trade + 10 Market Impact T + 10	Effective Spread − Market Impact = Observed Realized Spread T + 8	Effective Spread − Market Impact = Observed Realized Spread T + 10
Buys NO Brk IDs	0.01253	0.00144	0.00142	0.01026	0.01007
Buys Public Brk IDs	0.02578	0.00308	0.00312	0.02138	0.02101
Sells NO Brk IDs	−0.00281	−0.00149	−0.0016	−0.00127	−0.00115
Sells Public Brk IDs	−0.00334	−0.0024	−0.00265	−0.00086	−0.00060

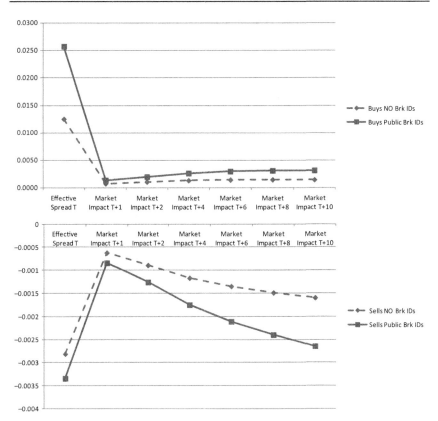

The figure shows the average univariate effective spread, and trade by trade market impacts for all aggregated sample stocks, separately for buyer- and seller-initiated trades, and for the pre (dotted line) and post (solid line) broker ID transparency periods (20 days prior and 20 days post October 25, 1999, with a month of omitted adjustment period). The trade impacts are expressed as relative ratios to the mid-point and in trade time for 1, 2, 4, 6, 8 and 10 trades after the current transaction.

The World's Most Transparent LOB

THE GLOSTEN–MILGROM AND KYLE MODELS

Assignment

— Please carry out the following assignments with style, quality and clarity of expression.

— Summarize the literature with focus on your specific area of interest, 1–3 pages, 10% of marks for this assignment

— Redefine the research question of the paper according to your own preferences and observations. Aim to sharpen the research question, improve or change the hypothesis, Tip: Apply what we are learning from the book about current, market developments and data availability, etc. Being innovative and thinking outside of the box will be reward! 30%

— Propose a suitable methodology for the research task. 15%

— Propose and define a suitable (empirical) data set to use for this study, data may be local, international, real market, simulated or survey based. 15%

— Clearly justify the additional contribution your research would provide to the literature. 20%

Models

Market microstructure

— Market microstructure studies the details of how markets work.
— Market microstructure is not neoclassical finance.
— Often directly opposes Efficient Market Hypothesis.
— If you believe markets are efficient:

  o the details of how markets work are irrelevant since...
  o you always get efficient price (less universally-known fee).

— Thus, microstructure embraces:

  o the possibility of short-term alpha; and
  o behavioral effects.

— Today we will consider models for microstructure phenomena.
— For these models need to adopt a different perspective.
— Models are simple; lets us conduct controlled experiments.

  o Eliminate all but one or two major factors.
  o Question: Does this model reproduce real-life features?

— If so: factors we are considering probably matter.
— We may even have an idea about how those factors matter.
— Less confusion about what matters helps build better models.
— Newest research combining such models with time series.
— *All models are wrong; some models are useful.*
— *George Box.*
— We will examine two asymmetric information models.

  o Asymmetry: Trades may contain private information.

— Sequential trade: independent sequence of traders.

  o Traders: informed (know asset value) or not; trade once.
  o Single market maker (MM); learns information by trading.

— Strategic trader: one informed trader can trade many times.

  o Informed trader considers own impact on later trades.
  o Uninformed (noise) traders also submit orders.
  o Single MM sees combined order, sets price and lls order.

The Glosten–Milgrom (1985) Model

The first important model of the bid–ask spread

— Most famous sequential trade model.
— MM quotes a bid B and ask A.
— Security has value $V = V_{\text{LOW}}$ or $V^{\text{HIGH}}, V_{\text{LOW}} < V^{\text{HIGH}}$.
— At time $t = 0$, informed traders (only) learn V.
— Time is discretized.
— Trades are for one unit, occur at each time step.
— MM has infinite capital: no inventory/bankruptcy concerns.

Condensed Derivation and Simulation

— See Insert by D. Rosenthal, University of Illinois Chicago, pp. 9–17.

Summary

— Basic idea: Spreads exist due to adverse selection.
— Buys/sells are unbalanced; but, price series is a martingale.
— Orders are serially correlated: buys tend to follow buys.

  ○ This and the preceding line seem contradictory.

— Trades have price impact: a buy increases B and A.
— Spreads tend to decline over time as MMs figure out V.
— Bid-ask may be such that market effectively shuts down.
— If uninformed were price-sensitive, spreads would be wider.
— Fun: Add very rare third trader, government, who always buys at V.
— Stunning: still converging after 50,000 trades.

The Kyle (1985) Model

The Kyle model provides a tractable framework in which liquidity and the informativeness of prices can be measured. It has played a key role in research on heterogeneous information in financial markets. The model formalizes the relation of liquidity to the average rate of flow of new information. The model has a discrete-time and a continuous-time version.

— Kyle, A.S., 1985, Continuous Auctions and Insider Trading, *Econometrica*, 53, 1315–1335.
— Cited 6,574 times and counting.

Continuous auctions and insider trading

By ALBERT S. KYLE (did this research at Monash and Yale)

— A dynamic model of insider trading with sequential auctions, structured to resemble a sequential equilibrium, is used to examine the informational content of prices, the liquidity characteristics of a speculative market and the value of private information to an insider The model has three kinds of traders: a single risk-neutral insider, random noise traders and competitive risk-neutral MMs. The insider makes positive profits by exploiting his monopoly power optimally in a dynamic context, where noise trading provides camouflage which conceals his trading from MMs. As the time interval between auctions goes to zero, a limiting model of continuous trading is obtained. In this equilibrium, prices follow Brownian motion, the depth of the market is constant over time, and all private information is incorporated into prices by the end of trading.

— Uninformed trades arrive as a Brownian motion and MMs see only the order imbalance.

— A dynamic model in which a trader with inside information will maximize his profits by trading gradually rather than trading all at once. The purpose of the paper is to answer questions such as the following:

   ○ How quickly is new private information incorporated into price?
   ○ How valuable is private information to an insider?
   ○ How does noise trading affect the volatility of prices? (Noise traders are those with no access to private information)
   ○ What determines the liquidity of a speculative market?

— The informed traders is more rational than in Glosten–Milgrom as they know their trading will impact prices. The optimal strategy for an informed trader is to conceal his trading amongst the trades of noise traders.

— The building blocks of Kyle's rather intricate model

 o Quantity traded by noise traders $\sim \mu$ normally distributed mean zero variance σ^2
 o Quantity traded by insider $\sim x$
 o The insider's trading strategy X
 o The MM's pricing rule P
 o *An equilibrium is defined as a pair X,P such that the following two conditions hold:*

  • *Profit Maximization (of alternative strategies informed trader will choose the one with largest profit vs. noise traders)*
  • *Market Efficiency (X,P will be chosen to accommodated random market price p)*

— The building blocks of Kyle's rather intricate model

 o *Four theorems are developed to accommodate*

  • *A single auction equilibrium*
  • *A sequential auction equilibrium*
  • *A continuous auction equilibrium*
  • *A convergence results single $\rightarrow$ continuous*

Condensed derivation and simulation

— See Insert By D. Rosenthal, University of Illinois Chicago pp. 20–35.

A few details nobody has previously noted

— Informed orders are larger after negative uninformed trades.
— Informed orders decrease after larger net orders, price moves.
— Recall: one leads to the other; confounding lives here.
— Informed order size increases slightly with time.
— Trade price moves toward the true value.
— Trade price may not converge to true value by end of trading.
— The appeal of Kyle (1985) is its applicability to real world markets and the terminology is used, for example, "noise traders in the spirit of Black and Kyle (1985)".

— Kyle's lambda, λ, is a widely used term for illiquidity. Measures value uncertainty vs. noise order uncertainty!

Recent Work

Econometrica, Vol. 72, No. 2 (March, 2004), 433–465.

Information in securities markets: Kyle Meets Glosten and Milgrom By Kerry Back and Shmuel Baruch

— This paper analyzes models of securities markets with a single strategic informed trader and competitive MMs. In one version, uninformed trades arrive as a Brownian motion and MMs see only the order imbalance, as in Kyle (1985). In the other version, uninformed trades arrive as a Poisson process and MMs see individual trades. This is similar to the Glosten–Milgrom (1985) model, except that we allow the informed trader to optimize his times of trading. We show there is an equilibrium in the Glosten–Milgrom-type model in which the informed trader plays a mixed strategy (a point process with stochastic intensity). In this equilibrium, informed and uninformed trades arrive probabilistically, as Glosten and Milgrom assume. We study a sequence of such markets in which uninformed trades become smaller and arrive more frequently, approximating a Brownian motion. We show that the equilibria of the Glosten–Milgrom model converge to the equilibrium of the Kyle model.

Printed in the United States
By Bookmasters